Critical AI in K–12 Classrooms

Critical AI in K-12 Classrooms

A Practical Guide for Cultivating Justice and Joy

STEPHANIE SMITH BUDHAI
MARIE K. HEATH

Harvard Education Press
Cambridge, Massachusetts

Paperback ISBN 9798895570180

The Library of Congress Cataloging-in-Publication Data is on file.

Published by Harvard Education Press,
an imprint of the Harvard Education Publishing Group

Harvard Education Press
8 Story Street
Cambridge, MA 02138

Cover by Dave Kessler Design

The typefaces in this book are Carrara and Gotham.

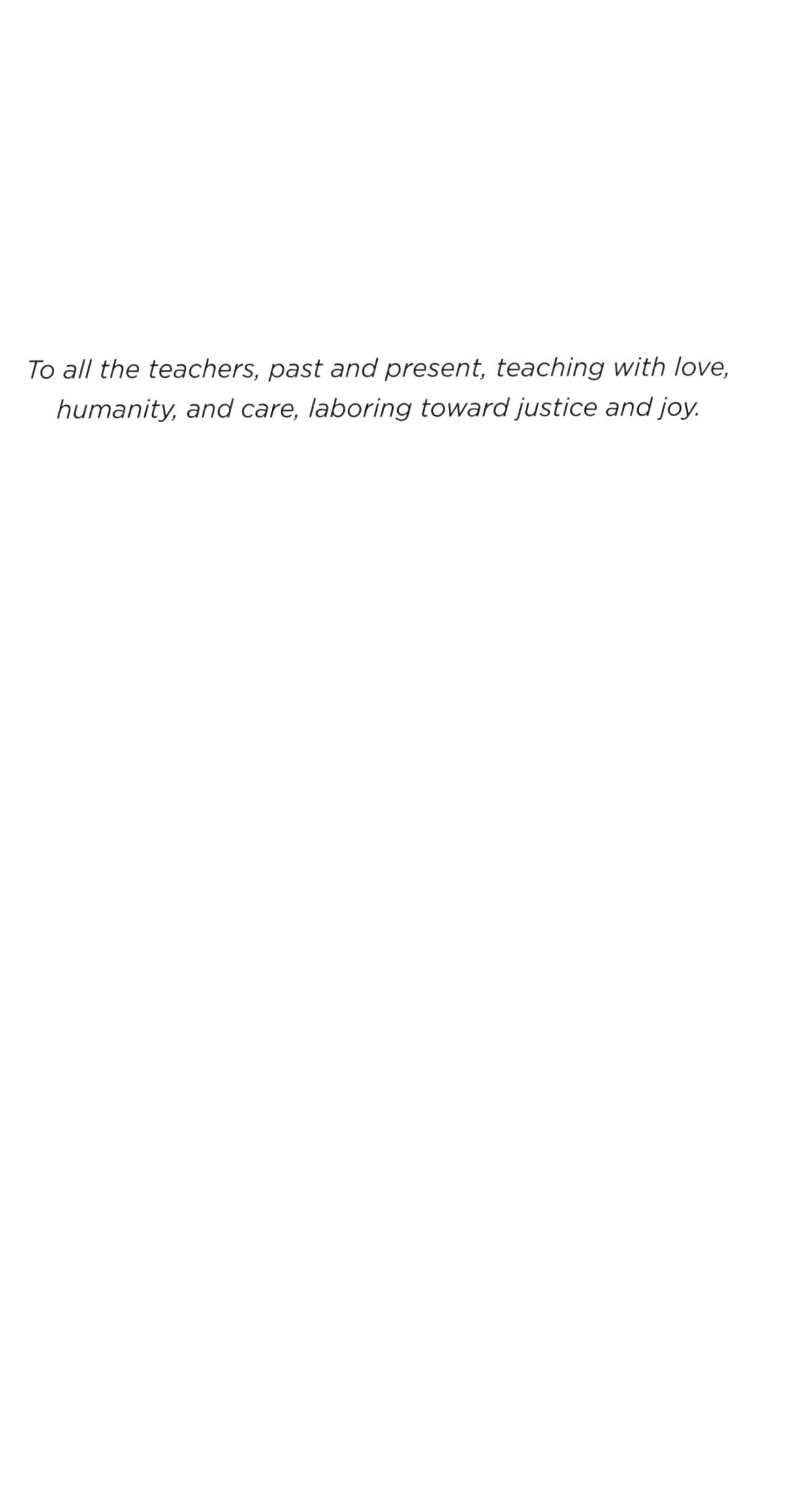

To all the teachers, past and present, teaching with love, humanity, and care, laboring toward justice and joy.

CONTENTS

FOREWORD

> Technology is not neutral. We're inside of what we make, and it's inside of us. We're living in a world of connections—and it matters which ones get made and unmade.
>
> —Donna Haraway, "A Cyborg Manifesto"[1]

WE HAVE BEEN LIVING in an AI-saturated world for decades, though we're only now becoming acutely aware of it. The release of ChatGPT, despite questions about the ethics of deploying such a transformative yet unfinished technology, has brought this reality into sharp focus. Suddenly AI seems to be everywhere, with boosters claiming it's "transforming whole industries" and warning that educational systems risk obsolescence if they don't rapidly embrace this new technology. This perceived inevitability narrative demands to be questioned, even as *AI literacy* becomes the new buzzword in education, spawning multiple frameworks to guide students, teachers, leaders, and parents.

While the transformative potential of AI is undeniable, the narrative of inevitability often prevents us from asking deeper, more troubling questions. These range from immediate concerns about authorship and intellectual property of the content used to train these models, to broader societal implications that we are only beginning to grasp. The environmental costs of training large language models are staggering, while the human costs—often borne by workers from the global south who must engage with toxic content to create AI guardrails—remain hidden from view. In an already fragmented social world, the rise of synthetic content and AI-generated artifacts threatens to further erode our shared sense of reality. The technology that promises to connect us may deepen our isolation, replacing authentic human relationships with pseudointeractions in an already lonely world. The gee-whiz tools that can create art and solve complex problems can also generate sophisticated misinformation and deepen social divisions. These tensions and contradictions demand our attention, even as we marvel at AI's capabilities.

As we confront these complexities, we need to develop a new understanding of what it means to live and learn in an AI-mediated world. This goes beyond merely using AI tools or understanding their functionality—it must encompass a broader collection of skills, competencies, and knowledge that allow us to thoughtfully engage with these technologies and their profound social and ethical implications. Such engagement requires us to recognize and interrogate the historical, social, and cultural contexts within which these technologies emerge and assert their dominance—contexts that often remain unexamined in our rush to adoption and implementation, contexts that fundamentally shape not just how we use these tools but how we understand ourselves and value our world.

What we need, therefore, is a reconceptualization of what it means to be literate in this new world. A particularly illuminating framework comes from a definition of literacy first put forth by Myers, "the ability to consciously subvert signs." As Myers argues, literacy is

> more than just the ability to use sign systems to communicate some conventional meaning, because . . . literacy should be reserved for some state of agency in which one can control, even manipulate, how signs are used to name and value the world. . . . The ability to subvert signs could only result from a continual self-examination of the underlying intertexts and ideologies that contextualize possible meanings, identities, and relationships within socially constructed practices.[2]

This conceptualization offers several crucial insights for understanding AI literacy. First, it emphasizes that AI systems are fundamentally about the manipulation of abstract signs and symbols—from language and images to code and data. Second, it foregrounds human agency—our ability to consciously direct these systems toward our own purposes. Third, it implies that AI systems, despite their complexity, are not sacrosanct but rather human constructions that can be redesigned and repurposed. Fourth, it highlights the importance of expertise, since meaningful subversion requires understanding which aspects of these systems can be bent, redirected, or reimagined. Finally, and perhaps most importantly, it places creativity at the center of literacy. The wicked problems we face in our relationship with AI demand creative solutions, especially since most AI systems are not designed with education or social justice in mind, requiring us to thoughtfully repurpose them for these crucial ends.

To understand what such conscious subversion looks like in practice—and what it might mean for AI literacy—I point to three examples across different domains of human creativity and resistance. These examples, drawn from art (Diego Rivera), popular culture (skateboarding), and education (Paulo Freire) illuminate diverse pathways toward creative resistance. These vignettes make the case that there is no one way forward, given the complexity of the world we live in. Our approaches must be eclectic, diverse, and organic, while sharing essential elements: deep systematic understanding, creative agency, and the kind of critical consciousness Myers describes—that continual self-examination of underlying ideologies and practices. It is recognizing the importance of these elements that can potentially transform tools of control into instruments of liberation.

Consider the Mexican muralist Diego Rivera, who consciously subverted the conventions of European artistic tradition to create a new visual language of social justice. Rivera's technical mastery of classical painting techniques became the foundation for radical innovation—transforming private gallery spaces into public forums, elite artistic conventions into tools for mass communication, and traditional artistic subjects into powerful representations of labor, struggle, and hope. His work demonstrates how deep understanding of a "style's" conventions enables its creative repurposing toward liberatory ends.

In skateboarding culture, this relationship between technical understanding and creative subversion is perhaps most joyfully embodied. Skateboarders read urban landscapes differently—seeing handrails not as mere supports but as opportunities for expression, empty pools not as abandoned spaces but as vessels of possibility. Their technical mastery of board and body allows them to transform the built environment into playgrounds of possibility. This community shows us how subversion can be both technically sophisticated and intrinsically joyful, how seeing the world differently enables us to reshape it.

And Paulo Freire's approach to literacy education offers another example of conscious subversion at work. By rejecting traditional literacy primers in favor of generative words drawn from learners' lives, Freire subverted conventional pedagogical approaches and structures of power. His method required deep understanding of both literacy instruction and local context but deployed this knowledge toward liberation rather than mere compliance. In doing so, he demonstrated how educational practices, when consciously subverted, can transform from tools of oppression into instruments of empowerment through critical examination of the ideologies that shape educational practice.

These themes—conscious subversion, technical mastery coupled with creative agency, and liberatory educational practices—lie at the heart of *Critical AI in K–12 Classrooms: A Practical Guide for Cultivating Justice and Joy*. The book makes a significant contribution not just to our understanding of artificial intelligence in education, but also to our ability to thoughtfully and creatively act within, and transform, our AI-mediated educational spaces. Stephanie Smith Budhai and Marie K. Heath ground their discussion in a deep appreciation for both the technical and social dimensions of AI, while never losing sight of education's transformative potential. Like the examples above, which move us from art to play to education, from visual to physical to conceptual understanding, and from individual to communal to systematic change, this book charts a path forward. Their thoughtful and intentional integration of culturally sustaining, fugitive, and abolitionist pedagogies offers educators concrete pathways for reimagining AI not as a tool to be feared or uncritically embraced, but as a site for creative resistance and collective joy. In doing so, they remind us that true education—whether digital, artificial, or human—always carries within it the seeds of transformation.

—Punya Mishra
Associate Dean of Scholarship and Innovation
Mary Lou Fulton Teachers College at
Arizona State University

INTRODUCTION

The AI Creep in Education: From the Margins to Ubiquity

> Artificial intelligence will become a major human rights issue in the twenty-first century.
>
> —Safiya Noble, *Algorithms of Oppression*

ARTIFICIAL INTELLIGENCE ISN'T JUST a tool that can be picked up and put down when we are finished using it. Technologies, including AI, exist in the time, space, and fabric of our social lives, weaving themselves into our world, and forever altering it. Early cameras, a technology of light and mirrors, were built to realistically capture a moment in time and reproduce it on film. Soon after the camera's invention, photographic images captured the imagination of people living in the late nineteenth century, and small trading cards of photographs, *cartes de visites*, became popular collector items. Pictures of leaders, soldiers, and US Civil War battle scenes were reproduced and shared during the time of so-called *cartomania*,[1] allowing for sentimental photos of sweethearts and powerful advertising for politicians.

Sojourner Truth, the self-emancipated abolitionist, women's rights activist, and foremother of Black feminism, reimagined and harnessed the power of the new technology of photography, with the aim of repurposing the technology toward justice. While the technology of the camera was predominately used by and for white people to reproduce and share their lives on film, Sojourner Truth recognized the power of images, and in particular, her own image. Ingeniously, she sold photographs of herself, clothed in the garments of the upper middle-class white women of her time, engaged in the dignity of women's work—for instance, while she was knitting—in order to raise money to fund the abolitionist cause. Technically, the photographer, not the person in the image, owned the photograph, so she added the line "I sell the shadow to support the substance" to each of her *cartes de visites*, in order to proclaim who she was and how she employed the profits of her image for freedom.

In this book, *Critical AI in K–12 Classrooms*, we hope you will join us in cleverly repurposing, reimagining, reclaiming, and when necessary, resisting the popular technology of our day: artificial intelligence. Inspired by activists like Sojourner Truth, we draw on culturally sustaining, fugitive, and abolitionist pedagogies to offer activities for K–12 educators to use in classrooms in order to work toward a more just world.

Sojourner Truth's reclaiming of the technology of the camera is not the only time the camera has intersected with issues of race. Since their invention, cameras have failed to effectively see dark skin. Taking a photo of darker skinned people has long required compensatory practices of lighting and makeup. The white people who designed and tested the technology of the camera neither included nor considered the ways their technological design might refuse to see darker skinned people.[2] Although the camera was invented in the nineteenth century, it was not until the tail end of the twentieth century that film was able to capture a lighter skinned and darker skinned person in the same photo, without substantial compensatory practices.

The long tail of the racism embedded in the technology of cameras continues to wag the technological dog today. The digital cameras on our phones long struggled to correctly capture and represent rich shades of skin. The facial recognition on our phones, powered by artificial intelligence, could not effectively see darker skinned individuals, and made it difficult to operate features on the phone powered by the face. Only a few years ago, in 2021, Google proudly advertised that their phones could finally see and portray darker skinned faces.[3] But even this came at a cost. In order to develop the dataset which taught the artificial intelligence to recognize a Black face, Google manipulated unhoused Black people living in Atlanta to give up their biometric likeness so that Google could develop a larger dataset of Black faces.[4]

So what can we do when technological advancement, even that tied to racial equity—like cameras that can finally see a range of skin tones—is encoded with bias? This book offers a way forward for teachers and students to navigate the complicated intersection of artificial intelligence, education, and justice.

OUR COLLECTIVE JOURNEY TOWARD JUST AI

We both began our careers as PK–12 teachers. Stephanie started in special education and Marie in secondary social studies. As the field of special education grew out of the civil rights movement, Stephanie's work with assistive technologies served as a catalyst in understanding the power of technology to impact and shape lives. For people without disabilities, technology can make life easier. But for people with disabilities, technology, when used responsibly and intentionally to support the needs of all people, serves a more vital role: it creates opportunities for equitable access in every aspect of life. This sentiment continues to inform Stephanie's approach to educational technology. In Marie's early career in social studies, she focused on developing young people to grow into citizens who take constructive actions for democracy. A large part of this work required understanding how technologies like social media influence young people's individual and collective lives. For instance, she has taught and researched the ways social media has fomented polarization, spread mis- and disinformation, altered young people's brains, and injured their mental health.

Our approaches and lenses to technology are entwined with our critical consciousness and justice-centered pedagogies, which we have developed and continue to develop across our professional and personal lives. These lenses and approaches, which we'll discuss more in chapter 3, have shaped our worldviews and have allowed us to understand technology as containing powerful forces which act on our lives—sometimes forces that gift equitable opportunity, and sometimes forces that steal it away from us. With the advent of generative AI, we recognize the world in which our students live and learn will irrevocably change. Students will use generative AI in their lives and in their schools. We would like them to be able to use it toward just ends. Thus, we ground this book, our teaching, and our professional work in our beliefs about technology and our commitments to justice.

WHY THIS BOOK? WHY NOW?

Education and technology are both touted as great social equalizers. Public schools work toward stronger and more just democracies, facilitate economic uplift, and empower students to see, understand, and change the world around them. Similarly, technology offers opportunities for humans to lead more equitable lives. AI technologies have helped identify disease in earlier and more treatable stages, recreated individual human voices for people who have lost their ability to speak due to disability, and other assistive technologies support disabled people and facilitate access and engagement in ever more inclusive ways.

However, despite their possibilities, schools are also sites of institutional injustice, rooted in a foundation intended to benefit dominant social groups while excluding, oppressing, and marginalizing others. The historic roots of injustices in schools reach across time, wrapping themselves around the educational lives of today's children, evidenced through disproportionately high disciplinary rates of Black girls,[5] standardized testing designed to measure ability but which actually produces results correlated to poverty and race,[6] the de facto segregation of US public schools,[7] and the attempted erasure of Indigenous languages and culture.[8]

Despite these injustices, Black, disabled, queer, and other marginalized children have braved angry mobs and navigated daily inequities in order to access free and equal public education. Similarly, marginalized teachers have developed powerful pedagogies of justice, resistance, and hope in order to ensure that students might engage with the power of education, despite the injustices embedded in the institution of schooling. Through the justice-oriented actions of these educators and students we may understand that, though the past may be prologue, it need not be destiny.

The same roots of injustice twining themselves around schooling similarly force themselves into technological design. For instance, AI as it currently exists in society has caused material harm to Black, queer, disabled, low-income, and other marginalized people. AI used by police misidentifies darker skinned faces, leading to false arrests, AI used in banking denies financial opportunities to people of color and women, and AI used in hiring practices refuses to consider women's resumes as suitable for jobs.[9]

Currently, K–12 educators are bombarded with conflicting and feverish messages about AI, all suggesting that educators must race to implement it before they "fall behind." However, few of these calls urging the rapid uptake of AI consider issues of racial equity or potential downsides and harms, nor do they emphasize justice-centered approaches. If teachers must integrate a technology we know can be damaging into schools, which can further that damage, then we encourage educators to lean on the wisdom and practice of teachers who have long found ways to work and thrive within oppressive spaces.

As educators and school systems race to develop policy and integrate AI into education, we find a dearth of materials which center *both* justice and educational technologies, and certainly very few which consider justice and generative AI. Thus, we wrote this book to address the absence of justice-centered AI in education literature and to provide educators with content that centers nonharmful and justice-oriented teaching. To do this, *Critical AI in K–12 Classrooms* draws on culturally sustaining,[10] fugitive,[11] and abolitionist pedagogies[12] to offer K–12 educators, educational administrators, teacher educators, scholars, and policy makers powerful approaches to just and joyful integrations of AI in education.

DEFINING AI

The concept of artificial intelligence, or AI, has captured the imagination of humans in different forms across time. Ever since Alan Turing coined the term *machine intelligence* in the mid-twentieth century, AI has specifically referred to computing algorithms. Several different types of AI exist, among them machine learning, large language models, natural language processing, and generative AI. (Note: this is not an exhaustive list, but for the purposes of the ways in which we will use the term AI in the book, these are the terms which are necessary to define and differentiate.)

- *Machine Learning (ML)*: a broad field of study in computer science which refers to machines using algorithms to learn from datasets and extrapolate generalized conclusions. Machine learning may be unsupervised. In unsupervised learning, the machine identifies and labels the data, instead of relying on a human to label data. Spotify and Netflix use unsupervised machine learning to make recommendations to us, the users. These apps ingest our data (what we've previously listened to or watched, as well as our demographic information), then digest our choices through their algorithms (making calculations based off of how long we watched a show, how quickly we switched a song, and what our age, gender, race, and location are, among other inputs), in order to make a generalization (the app recommends a new artist or show).

- *Natural Language Processing (NLP)*: another broad field of study in computer science which aims to have machines interpret text and speech, as well as manipulate text and speech to replicate language patterns. Machines using NLP can "understand" written or spoken language. We use scare quotes here because NLPs do not actually understand language; rather, they have been taught the many rules of linguistics, including grammar, syntax, and semiotics, written as mathematical models (algorithms). Powerful NLP algorithms can summarize salient points, make inferences, and offer appropriate suggestions for what words would make sense when, for instance, drafting a text or email. If your email program has ever prompted you with a phrase, or your word processing program has underlined a potential grammar mistake, you have interacted with NLP.
- *Large Language Models (LLMs)*: Until recently, these models were too large for computers to store and process. These models require a vast and varied dataset comprising words, phrases, sentences, and paragraphs in a given language. The language dataset is ingested by the machine, and then digested through algorithms which rely upon intense processing power. While still physically, financially, and environmentally costly, advancements in hardware and software since 2020 have dramatically increased the number of LLMs.
- *Generative Artificial Intelligence (genAI)*: Generative AI combines machine learning, natural language processing, and large language models in order to produce, or generate, complex text, speech, video, music, or images in response to questions. GenAI leans on the ML algorithms of unsupervised learning, the databases of LLMs, and the tools of NLPs. Popular platforms like ChatGPT, DALL-E, Midjourney, and Firefly are all examples of generative AIs. As of this book's publication, in 2025, most people referring to AI tend to mean genAI.

There has been a call for research and action that addresses the inherent risks and harm related to using AI technologies. In 2021, before the wider release of large language models (LLMs) to the public, Dr. Emily Bender, a linguist and professor at the University of Washington, and her colleagues cautioned the field of computer science to pause and evaluate the risks of ever larger language models for society.[13] They enumerated the injustices that could ensue if LLMs were to become too large. Specifically, they noted the hegemonic viewpoints embedded in the vast dataset of *all of the internet.* Further, they emphasized the importance of understanding how LLMs work and the importance of educating scholars and the public on how algorithms work. They were concerned that without understanding how algorithms work, users could be misled into imagining the algorithm mathematics to find the best average of data. In *Critical AI in K–12 Classrooms,* we respond to this call, contributing to AI equity work by offering practical resources for educators to apply in K–12 teaching and learning environments.

INJUSTICE EMBEDDED IN AI

While generative AI and large language models may be relatively new to K–12 education, artificial intelligence such as algorithms, machine learning, and natural language processing (NLP) models have existed in society and schools for decades. Technology scholars, primarily Black women researching AI, have repeatedly identified the real and present danger that artificial intelligence is causing to minoritized people in their day-to-day lives.[14] For example, MIT graduate Dr. Joy Buolamwini found that companies like Microsoft, IBM, and Amazon designed facial recognition AI that misidentified women and people with darker skin at far higher rates.[15]

Unfortunately, these technologies are already being bought by police departments and used to (mis)identify and arrest darker skinned people.[16] Biased AI reproduces housing and lending inequities, prompting lenders to reject a higher percentage of loans and charge more interest to Black and Latinx applicants than white applicants.[17] Health-care workers using AI to predict health risks and outcomes routinely overlook the pain of

Black women, leading to underdiagnosis and increased death compared to their white counterparts.[18] Search engines using AI reinforce harmful stereotypes about Black bodies, especially Black female bodies, as companies like Google privilege profit over equity in their search algorithms.

Until Safiya Noble's book *Algorithms of Oppression: How Search Engines Reinforce Racism* exposed this practice, a Google search of "Black girls" prioritized hypersexualized images. The field of education is not exempt, and what we have described here are only a few disconcerting examples of the harm that AI has caused. In K–12 classrooms, algorithmically based programs like ClassDojo rely upon teachers to enter quantitative representations of qualitative student behavior in order to run an algorithm to identify how "good" a student's behavior is and to pass that information on to the student's subsequent teachers. Often, this reinforces dominant paradigms of expected behavior and harms students forced to the margins,[19] and perpetuates the long-standing overrepresentation of Black boys being disciplined for similar behaviors when compared to their white counterparts.[20] *Critical AI in K–12 Classrooms* captures these inequities, providing pathways for amelioration that supports justice and joy in AI use for K–12 students.

AI CRITICALITY

We cannot expect our students to become justice-oriented digital citizens with the skills to critically approach online content if we ourselves do not model a criticality in our engagement with technologies such as generative AI. Since 2022, AI has been consuming our collective imaginations, and much of the focus has centered on modifying existing digital tools to include AI or creating new AI digital tools geared for K–12 teaching and learning. Despite scholars like Emily Bender, Ruha Benjamin, Joy Buolamwini, Timnit Gebru, and others sounding alarms about technological injustice embedded in existing AI, powerful organizations influencing technology practices in education, including the International Society for

Technology in Education (ISTE) and the Association for Supervision and Curriculum Development (ASCD), have encouraged the adoption of AI in a range of teaching practices, publishing multiple resources and professional development courses ranging from what teachers can learn from generative AI, to how to use AI to write a lesson, to a range of AI based activities to use with students.[21]

Although these respected educational technology organizations and industry leaders have hastened to implement AI in education, there is scant research on the ways AI may promote and impact equitable education and inclusive learning. As educators and school systems race to develop policy and integrate AI into education, intentional integration in the use of AI to transform learning in nonharmful ways must be centered. This is where *Critical AI in K–12 Classrooms* positions itself to address the current field that is devoid of critically, particularly when it comes to generative AI in education.

The tendency toward hasty implementation despite little research-based practice reflects a long and problematic trend in education technology practice and scholarship.[22] For instance, school systems rapidly adopted Google products, not questioning how Google might be taking advantage of underfunded public schools while offering free or low-cost technology, hardware, and learning platforms. However, recently districts have become concerned about the ways Google harvests student data inside and outside of school, and have filed lawsuits against the company for violating the privacy rights of children.[23] In addition to unjust data practices, the use of corporate technologies in education nudges pedagogical decisions through encoded biases and behaviorist tendencies in design, frequently harming the most vulnerable students in school systems.[24]

Similar to Bender and her colleagues' call to computer science, critical educational technology scholars have asked the field to pause before rushing technologies in front of children, and instead consider whether the futures the technologies promise are the futures that we genuinely desire.[25] Educators face challenges when considering the implementation of LLMs in learning, given the current and possible harms of AI and LLMs, and faced with insufficient research-based findings on the use of AI tools and environments on marginalized students. Like Bender and colleagues, we are confident this is the time to engage with AI in education, before practices become ingrained, calcified, or otherwise allow for a post hoc discovery of harms and risks.

CONTINUED RELEVANCE OF THIS BOOK AS AI ADVANCES

Technology changes, and it changes fast. We recognize that in some ways, even by the time this book is published, some people may consider what we have written about generative AI already to be old news. As with most technologies, predicting the next iteration of this technology is nearly impossible. While the technology of AI is central to this book, even more important is the ways we teach with and about it. Our scholarship and experiences shared in this book center the ways technologies impact (or fail to impact) education.

While we should be cautious when attending to the rapidly changing technological advances in the field, and in particular generative AI, we still believe it is important to provide teachers with guidance on its use. Our aim is that you will find *Critical AI in K–12 Classrooms* relevant now and will continue to find it relevant as AI advances. That is because this book applies evidence-based pedagogies of justice to AI use in K–12 classrooms, and couples them with a focus on the distinguishing features and impacts of AI, rather than on specific tools. The developers of generative AI technologies have already advanced its capabilities from the type and text-based version of ChatGPT that was released in initial public offerings just a few years ago. Now, users can develop new visual art and video, create songs, modify their speech and voices, view and analyze art, and have generative AI talk out loud in conversation with them.

The AI technological landscape will shift, but teachings with and about AI, grounded in justice, will remain relevant and necessary with each technological change. Thus, our book focuses not on specific brand name technologies but rather on the pedagogical dispositions and strategies that teachers can utilize when incorporating AI technologies in teaching and learning. The purpose of *Critical AI in K–12 Classrooms* is to offer teachers a reference on how to make sense of these changes. In other words, how to recognize the accuracy and ethics of the newly created content, and how to use evidence-based pedagogical techniques to engage with generative AI in safe and productive ways. Therefore, as new AI technologies inevitably emerge, teachers can transfer the content from this book to those technologies.

Bringing a justice-centered lens to the work of educational technology and using generative AI in K–12 classrooms is a necessity that will not only stand the test of time but will also lay a foundation to address future advances of AI—a future we may not even be able to imagine. However, the dispositions and pedagogies within *Critical AI in K–12 Classrooms* will be here to anchor educators no matter what unforeseen technological changes may come our way.

AIMS AND ORGANIZATION OF *CRITICAL AI*

This book is guided by the overarching question, "How can we prepare teachers to both understand and use AI toward justice and joy, and in ways that do not harm marginalized and minoritized students?" To answer this question, *Critical AI in K–12 Classrooms* will show readers how to do the following:

1. Name and acknowledge existing injustice in AI and schools
2. Develop and lean into mind-sets of critical consciousness and technoskepticism
3. Apply culturally sustaining, fugitive, and abolitionist pedagogies to teach judiciously with and about AI

4. Take action in personal, pedagogical, professional, and participatory domains.

We numbered these items because there is some linearity to this work. We have to name existing injustices so that we know what types of injustice we are resisting. We have to develop knowledge, skills, and dispositions toward justice around technology and education. We have to identify specific and evidence-based pedagogies that we can then apply to technology in education. Finally, as abolitionist teachers, we are committed to making change inside and outside of school, in the spaces where we hold power in our personal lives, in our pedagogies, in our professional domains, and through collective participatory actions. We also emphasize that despite the progression, this is not a checklist and no step can ever be fully finished. We will always be learning more about injustice and how to teach for a more just world, so each area is worth returning to and reflecting upon as we grow as professionals.

Critical AI in K–12 Classrooms addresses each of these components through six chapters and a conclusion. The book opens with a brief history of AI and its uses and misuses in education. Next, we provide concrete examples of strategies and mind-sets that help educators confront the injustices embedded in schools and technologies. Then, we lean into established types of pedagogy, including *culturally sustaining*, *fugitive*, and *abolitionist* in order to apply them to teaching with and about AI. Finally, we offer practical and actionable ways to practice these frameworks for educators, scholars, teacher educators, educational technology professionals, and school administrators in order to use AI technology in just and equitable ways.

Chapter 1, "Harms of AI: Data and Algorithmic Injustice," centers the harm that AI has caused in myriad facets of society and in education. We highlight the embedded injustice in the data and coding of AI, arguing that its capabilities are impacted by the developers' biases, perspectives, and beliefs. Moreover, the data feeding generative AI is not representative of all people, gathered as it is from the predominantly global north users of the internet. This creates unfair, unethical, and unjust use of AI for communities of color and marginalized people.[26] In this chapter, we take a powerful stance, focusing on the discriminatory outcomes of AI while highlighting the peril associated with using AI technologies in learning. We offer examples of learning programs used in schools to meet academic measures, which can perpetuate long-standing prejudice and racism. Finally, we provide insights and examples for educators to reduce harm and impacts on students when using AI in the classroom.

In chapter 2, "Teaching Machines: What Was, What Is, What Might Be," we focus the AI discussion on its use in schools, highlighting perennial critiques of technologies in education. AI technologies have been present in the past, are here in the now, and will continue to evolve for future teaching and learning. This chapter also examines the intersection of AI in education with white supremacy, a world crippled by civil unrest, and a call for equity from marginalized groups. We close chapter 2 by framing two possible futures of AI use in education: *"Revolutionized" Education* and *The Revolution.*

Chapter 3, "Mind-Sets for Justice: Educator Knowledge and Dispositions Toward AI," transitions the book's focus from the storied histories and harmful uses of AI in society and schools to practical applications of what educators need to know and believe to ameliorate some of these concerns. This chapter focuses on developing mind-sets of critical consciousness and technoskepticism. If teachers are not familiar with AI, their mind-sets toward it may be unduly influenced by dominant Silicon Valley narratives of technological inevitability and progress, instead of being grounded in notions of powerful justice and education.

We argue that given the prevalence of AI use in education, all educators must have baseline knowledge regarding what AI is and how it works in order to make informed pedagogical decisions about when and how to use AI in the classroom, even if they do not have any background in algorithmic measures. We provide vocabulary, content, and examples that introduce educators to frameworks centering justice-based approaches to AI, which we term JustAI. These include *discriminatory design,*[27] *technoskepticism,*[28] and *weapons of math destruction.*[29] Applying these frameworks helps educators develop dispositions and mind-sets toward just AI use in schools.

In chapter 4, "Creating Homeplace: Culturally Relevant, Responsive, and Sustaining Pedagogies for Inclusive AI," we build on previous chapters' discussion of AI's unequal harmful impacts on society's most vulnerable individuals, and provide asset-based approaches that educators can leverage when using AI. We introduce bell hooks' concept of *homeplace*[30] to prepare our classrooms as places of hope and nurturing, and as sites of resistance. In doing this, we present culturally relevant, responsive, and sustaining pedagogies as powerful ways forward to craft and facilitate lessons that include teaching with and about AI. We also lean into the work that teachers in K–12 classrooms are carrying out, and share vignettes of practice throughout this chapter, connecting research to practical applications in the field.

Chapter 5, "Making Good, Necessary Trouble: Resisting and Rebuilding Through Fugitive and Abolitionist Pedagogies," turns toward John Lewis' *good trouble* as a North Star to guide the actions and pedagogies we propose within larger community settings. Marginalized educators and students, as well as nonmarginalized allies in school systems, have long histories of teaching toward justice in the midst of oppression. We draw on two of these pedagogical practices, fugitive[31] and abolitionist,[32] to offer learning activities that lift up joyful resisting and rebuilding. We close with suggested learning activities which challenge injustice and work to reclaim AI technologies toward more equitable ends.

In chapter 6, "Toward JustAI: Taking Personal, Professional, Pedagogical, and Participatory Action," offer action items to make change toward more justice in and with AI. We have developed four areas for enacting change: the personal, the pedagogical, the professional, and the participatory (or collective), which are inspired by the work of Patricia Hill

Collins.[33] In each of these four domains we provide clear and actionable examples you can take to make change toward a more just use of AI.

In the conclusion, "Moving Forward: The Future of JustAI," we acknowledge that AI has inherent flaws; however, we remain hopeful that through good struggle and the powerful pedagogy presented in the book, educators can democratize AI technologies, but also teach students methods for judiciously and joyfully engaging with AI. We discuss what the future may hold for AI use in education, centering the continuance of contributing to the good struggle in using *Critical AI in K–12 Classrooms,* and we ponder what AI in the future may mean for teachers and students. We suggest that, when the pedagogies that we share in this book are anchored in the wisdom of marginalized educators, we can better navigate the incessant technological shifts the future will hold.

1

Harms of AI: Data and Algorithmic Injustice

> Success in creating AI could be the biggest event in the history of our civilization. But it could also be the last—unless we learn how to avoid the risks. Alongside the benefits, AI will also bring dangers like powerful autonomous weapons or new ways for the few to oppress the many.
>
> —Stephen Hawking, October 19, 2016, at the launch of the £10 million Leverhulme Centre for the Future of Intelligence

SO, IS AI HARMFUL?

AI exists everywhere, but perhaps the greatest trick AI has ever played is to convince us that it doesn't. AI accompanies us throughout our waking days and sleeping nights, a seamless partner who listens to our heartbeats, tells us when we are in a REM dream state, navigates us across our neighborhoods, discovers new songs for us that we are delighted to learn we enjoy, recommends products for us to buy, develops learning objectives and designs active learning lessons for us to teach to our students, and listens for our voices to turn on lights, send a message to our children, or talk to the delivery person on the other side of our door. In almost every facet of our lives, our homes, cars, schools, the news, or conversations, AI seamlessly calculates and predicts what it thinks we need.[1] AI has turned itself into such a helpful extension of our human selves that, like the most attentive and discreet human assistant, it makes itself necessary for our daily functioning while remaining unobtrusively on the borders of our field of vision.

And yet, paradoxically, we seem to be obsessed with AI. Our collective imagination centers on the transformational elements of AI technologies, offering up a binary view of AI as either savior or slayer. As Dr. Ruha Benjamin, MacArthur Fellow and professor of African American studies at Princeton points out, both of these metaphors are pushed on us by technology corporations and the media.[2] Admittedly, it is effortless and quite comfortable, and perhaps even *comforting*, to visualize the efficacious possibilities of a savior AI. AI will solve climate change. AI will fix education and finally (finally!) create time for teachers to do the work of teaching. AI will streamline children's bus routes to school and offer us driverless cars whenever we need them. Similarly, we collectively tend to imagine the ways AI will become our slayer—a sci-fi future of Frankenstein's monsters, robot overlords who turned on their human creators. The advent of generative AI has hastened these binary predictions. It is a different beast. Its complex and multifaceted ability to create poetry, design images, compose music, interpret photographs, grade student work, and engage in lengthy conversation has captured our attention and stunned us with its powerful abilities.

As we move forward in our thinking around AI, it becomes clear that how we imagine AI and its uses in education is, unfortunately in many ways, dictated by technology companies. They have designed a powerful technology which can generate humanlike thought, conversation, and art, as if by magic. We are told the future is inevitable, that the AI genie is out of the bottle, and that we must learn to live with it or fall behind. The technology companies' imagined futures for society become our imagined future. Their imagined future for education becomes our imagined future. Consequently, our attention toward the extremes also distracts us from truly seeing and examining the quiet AI assistant which lurks around us in our day to day. An obsession with the extremes prevents us from asking critical questions to determine whether programs, owned by multi-billion dollar companies, should have access to our inner minds and bodies; whether the algorithms, designed by a majority of *pale males* (a term coined by AI researcher Joy Buolamwini to highlight the overwhelming whiteness and maleness of the coding workforce), might carry within them the implicit bias of majoritarian views; and whether complex social, environmental, and educational problems can be solved by the silver bullet of technology.

For AI to be powerful, synthetic intelligence needs access to actual intelligence. It wants to know us, so that it can be the best artificial us. When we interact with generative AI, it works to figure out our story—who we are, what we desire—so that it can better understand us and provide us with the information we are seeking (or, the information it calculates we are seeking). When it learns us, it absorbs our foibles, our mistakes, and our implicit biases. The biased and targeted information that AI absorbs is reason to pause and consider its potential harms. This learning that AI does is not just in one part of our lives, it is everywhere, in our homes, schools, and communities. Consequently, while the field of K–12 education may be seen as a microcosm of larger society, how AI is used and impacts modernity and evolutionary constructs of life, and what and how K–12 students learn regarding generative AI, is not inconsequential.

Despite discussions around AI in society, there has not been an equivalent focus on AI in education.[3] In fact, a quick Google search for "harms of AI" resulted in issues such as transparency, privacy concerns, ethics, dependence on AI, security, existential risks, job placement, job loss, deepfakes, social manipulation, automation, and economic inequality, among others, including artificial intelligence itself being highlighted.[4] Yes, artificial intelligence itself was ironically named as a harm of AI. We must acknowledge that some of these resulting harms of AI can impact the families of students, at least in some peripheral way. For example, if families lose jobs because of AI technologies, then certainly this would have an impact on students' livelihoods, which may trickle down into their school performance. Similarly, if health professionals using AI technologies misdiagnose patients of color, or use incorrect algorithms to make medical decisions,[5] AI technologies are impacting students' and their families' lives. Although AI's harms extend to education and its stakeholders—students, teachers, their parents, families, and surrounding communities—we have a less concrete understanding of what these harms look like.

This era of AI is not the first time that discussions on the harms of technology in education have proliferated. Although educational technology applications have been seen as ways to support academic outcomes for students, concerns about isolation and decreased socialization as a result of prolonged individual use of technology have existed for almost a century, since the advent of the chalkboard in schools.[6] Particularly with adolescents, adults worry that increased screen time impacts both academic achievement and social outcomes.[7] In spite of these concerns, educators continue to critically consume educational technology, with a focus on generative AI and its related constructs.

We don't share all of these harms to say we should not use AI in education. Rather, we believe that peeling away corporate hype and understanding AI in schools and society is a necessary step to teaching with and about AI. With both generality and specificity, our discussion and arguments in this first chapter center the harms that AI has caused in society already, and its potential to do so even more in education spaces. To build context around how AI works and where the data comes from, we provide a brief, practitioner-structured overview of how AI is developed, breaking down how data is pulled from AI based on limited information, coded by humans who carry implicit bias within them. After, we move the discussion to discriminatory outcomes of AI in larger society, while drawing out the peril associated with using these AI technologies in education. As with the introduction of most new technologies, and specifically because of the interest, vastness, and capabilities of generative AI, we recognize that continued AI use in schools is probably inevitable. We do not want to shy away from this perennial reality, and instead we offer some positive impacts of using AI, providing practical examples that educators reading this book can use, while reducing the harms of AI and larger impacts on the students in your classrooms.

A BIT ON HOW AI WORKS

While the purpose of this book is not to explain in detail the science of artificial intelligence, it is important to briefly overview how AI works, and address the immediate implications of its use in school. Understanding how technology tools work within the context of education settings is an important part of teacher education and has been added to myriad coursework requirements for preservice teachers. Professional development workshops and training for in-service teachers have focused on using new technology tools in the classroom, and representatives from the technology industry clamor to attend conferences and conventions in expo halls and sessions with the hope of explaining how the educational technology tool they are representing works as well as the positive academic, social, and/or behavioral outcomes for students that can happen as a result of its use. Because AI is more powerful than other technologies that have been previously available in schools, we must not only become familiar with educational technology tools that have been modified to use AI technologies—such as the AI question generator that is available in the popular Kahoot! platform—but also with how technologies such as Gemini (formerly Google Bard), which was created specifically as a generative AI chatbot, operate, and the potential harms that exist as a result.

Technically speaking, AI is a machine. There are computer-mediated functionalities that work as a machine would. However, there is still a very humanistic component to AI that is sometimes overlooked in discussions. As we noted earlier, to be a powerful synthetic technological intelligence, the machine must appear as close as possible to authentic, human, intelligence. Thus, a central theme of this book utilizes a human-centered approach to AI which considers the values of dignity, justice, and human rights.[8]

Early on in our careers, when technology tools started to become popular in K–12 schools, language such as *teaching with technology* was prevalent. Teacher education coursework and books used the *teaching with technology* term, and in-service teachers were encouraged to partner with technology as if they were a co-teacher. As time went on, language around this changed, and *leveraging technology* or *using technology in teaching in learning* became more common. Technology can be used in teaching and learning under the guidance of teachers who use the functional capacities of technologies to carry out specific learning outcomes. This means that technology is not a neutral tool, and that, at the very least, we must understand background information regarding how the technology is created, how it operates, and how to expand its capacity and reach beyond the learning activities that we choose to leverage it for during use of it.

Given the extensive focus and push on its use in all facets of life, this leads us to where we are today with AI technologies. Teachers are bombarded with information about AI, what it is and is not doing, and especially about all the new AI educational technology tools that we should incorporate in our lessons. What we have not heard much of, as educators, is how AI works. This isn't surprising: most of us are not computer or data scientists. To understand how AI works at the most basic level means to start with people. More specifically, technology tools are not devoid of human capacity. As tech ethicist David Ryan Polgar shares on his website All Tech Is Human, AI technology actually relies on humans to work. When it is working, it is learning patterns and structures, and seeing regularities that have been imputed by humans based on their own lived experiences and vantage points. From there, AI is able to acquire new skills. But humans are flawed, messy, and not neutral. Humans have strong beliefs about how the world is, and about different groups of people, and those thoughts, perspectives, prejudices and biases are poured into their work: the codes, algorithms, and datasets. We will explore this in greater depth, but before we go further, it is important to understand these terms related to how AI works:

- *Algorithm*: a series of steps that are designed to instruct with the goal of a task being accomplished.[9]
- *Bias*: a preference for or against a person based on their race, gender, name, or other demographic characteristics.[10]
- *Data*: information stored and used within computer-mediated spaces for examination and to help with decision-making.[11]
- *Neural Network*: a model or machine learning program that uses the processes that mimic the way the human brain operates to make decisions.[12]

Biased Data Sets

The information (data) AI pulls from is created and influenced by the humans who are building the technology. As such, and because the developers of algorithms and codes are people, their biases, perspectives, and beliefs are intertwined. These humans who are mostly in the computer and data science fields are most likely to be white, able-bodied men. It is much less likely that a person working in a science, technology, engineering, or math (STEM) field is from a minoritized group. The National Science Foundation (NSF) has released data on underrepresented groups in STEM since 1977.[13] In 2023, the NSF released their *Diversity and STEM: Women, Minorities, and Persons with Disabilities 2023*, which indicated that Hispanic, Black, American Indian, and Alaska Native people made up 31 percent of the US population, but only 24 percent of the STEM workforce in 2021. Moreover, these groups were more likely to work in STEM fields that require technical skills or certification rather than in those that require a bachelor's degree or higher education. Women represented about one-third of the STEM workforce (35 percent). It is notable that their wages were consistently lower than men's.

Thus, AI learns from a small sector of the human population that is not representative of the diverse society as a whole. Increasing the racial diversity of STEM professionals is a long-standing issue which has yet to be resolved. And because of the underrepresentation of racial minorities and women in the computer and data science fields, discriminatory and racist underpinnings are laced into the fabric of how AI works. With generative AI specifically, new content is being created that may have not ever existed, and could be completely false, like deepfakes of voices, video footage, or other images. Simply put, the data that AI pulls from is embedded with injustices. This means that AI's capabilities are impacted. Just as our students are learning concepts in our classrooms, the technology tools that students use that have AI embedded in them are also looking for patterns and information, from which they then generate new images, words, music, and other creative pursuits.

AI learns algorithms in order to acquire the skills needed to complete a task, and to do so, it must pull information from somewhere; think about the neural network we defined above. According to an MIT news brief, "Neural nets are a means of doing machine learning, in which a computer learns to perform some task by analyzing training examples," and, "Modeled loosely on the human brain, a neural net consists of thousands or even millions of simple processing nodes that are densely interconnected."[14] The AI is trained on datasets, which over time are adjusted based on inputs that users provide. The issue here resides in the fact that women, people from lower socioeconomic groups, racial minorities, and other minoritized individuals are not always included in the datasets that AI uses. The data to a certain extent reflect their human coders, who have developed their perspectives based on their singular lived experiences. The data feeding generative AI is not representative of the people in society as a whole, and is gathered from the predominantly global north users of the internet. This creates unfair, unethical, and unjust use of AI for communities of color and marginalized people.[15] When biased and discriminatory information is represented online, this translates to AI pulling equally biased and discriminatory information to generate outputs. It is important to note that this lack of representation is a major harm of AI that exacerbates other harms. AI pulls from just a small subset of representative data, that is, only those data that are included in large language models for interpretation. Yet humans in other sectors of society, including education, make life-changing decisions based on it.

Unfair and Unethical Use of AI in Society

Since its inception, AI has led to powerful possibilities and unanticipated and unexpected consequences. For instance, in 1966, Joseph Weizenbaum, a computer scientist and professor at MIT, developed a natural language processing model, ELIZA, which "conversed" with humans by reflecting back the last several words or phrases that the human interlocutor typed into the machine. Despite the lack of complex data or speech patterns, humans almost immediately began to anthropomorphize the ELIZA machine, ascribing to it intelligence, feelings, desires, and other human traits. Weizenbaum found it astounding and disturbing that humans should form parasocial relationships with a machine which did not understand them, but merely parroted them. He spent the rest of his career parsing the differences between humans and machines and highlighting the politicization of math, science, and computing.[16]

THE DEFAULT SETTING OF AI IS INJUSTICE

Sixty years after ELIZA, natural language processing models like ChatGPT not only mimic speech, but they also access massive datasets which they draw on to generate conversational and informational responses. It now feels even more natural to engage in conversation and collaboration with AI. However, as computer scientists, mathematicians, and sociologists like Emily Bender, Joy Buolamwini, Timnit Gebru, Ruha Benjamin, Cathy O'Neil, Sasha Costanza-Chock, and Safiya Noble have noted, the datasets carry within them the encoded biases of the material world. The impact of data and algorithmic injustice shows up across industries and institutions.

For instance, in banking, lenders have used a predictive AI tool to offer loan terms to individuals. Despite being hailed as an opportunity to eliminate existing bias in lending practices, the algorithm led to higher interest rates and increased unfavorable terms for Black and Latinx borrowers.[17] The algorithms calculate loan rates based on data which reflect years of discriminatory practices. The residual impact of redlining, discriminatory housing practices, and de jure and de facto segregation have contaminated the seemingly "objective" data encoded into lending algorithms, inaccurately equating zip codes as a proxy for loan risk. When a lender inputs an applicant's information into the lending software, the software's algorithm is incapable of identifying and disaggregating the residue of historic injustice from the applicant's other qualifications. As a result, Black and Latino borrowers routinely pay a *racial premium* on their home loans due to increased interest rates compared to their white counterparts.[18] Similarly, credit card offers using algorithms offer more favorable options to men than women. Famously, when the Apple credit card debuted, it offered Apple founder Steve Wozniak ten times the credit offered to his wife, even though they share assets and had been married for years.[19]

Predatory companies have coupled the discriminatory practices of lending algorithms with social media marketing algorithms in order to target Latino users with false offers of the American dream in a new home. The US Department of Justice sued the home developer and lender Colony Ridge because they exploited Latino social media users.[20] The company offered predatory loans to immigrant borrowers through direct advertisement on social media sites. Then the company exploited language barriers, promising city services that did not exist and building homes that flooded with raw sewage.

In policing, AI has normalized surveillance and resulted in false arrests and the police shooting and killing of thirteen-year-old Adam Toledo in

2021. The AI software application PredPol claims to predict where and when crimes may take place. Police departments in cities across the US, including Chicago, Baltimore, Detroit, and L.A., use AI surveillance software like PredPol and ShotSpotter to determine locations and times to dispatch officers. PredPol will often predict multiple crimes per day in Black and Latino neighborhoods; however, it can sometimes go years before it predicts a crime will occur in whiter neighborhoods.[21] It recommends daily patrols around public housing and in communities which already have complicated and fraught relationships with policing. Despite the company's awareness that it might target Black and Latino residents up to four hundred times more frequently than white residents, it marketed its program to police agencies anyway.[22]

Police departments also use AI facial recognition software that has been proven to be ineffective at identifying women and darker skinned individuals. Unfortunately, this software has led to the false arrest of citizens in the US, all of them Black.[23] ShotSpotter, an AI powered software which "listens" on street corners for the sound of gunshots and then alerts police departments that it believes that someone has fired a weapon, was what resulted in the death of Adam Toledo when he was shot by police after they were directed to his location by the AI.[24]

Foreign governments have harnessed AI to effect social control. China uses an extensive system of data surveillance and artificial intelligence systems to monitor and nudge behaviors. The Chinese government collects billions of points of information, including geolocation, DNA, facial recognition, and voice prints, generating deeply personal profiles on individuals in order to track and control people.[25] China also uses its AI surveillance capabilities to detain, repress, terrorize, and force interment on the minority Muslim Uyghurs living in China.[26] While these specific authoritarian threats may be more likely to occur in countries lacking longer democratic traditions, it is not unimaginable to see parallel harms in other locations. Consider, for instance, that the data broker SafeGraph sold the data location of people who visited abortion clinics to whoever wished to purchase this information.[27] This data can be used by governments—for instance, the CDC purchased $420,000 worth of data from SafeGraph to analyze COVID-19 data—or by radical activists seeking to sow harm and discord.

In democratic countries with more stringent laws to protect civil liberties, it is companies that use their machine learning algorithms to influence social behavior. In a single day, Facebook was able to turn out an extra 340,000 people to vote in the 2010 US congressional election. The company used its powerful algorithm and massive reach to experiment on 61 million users, showing different ads to different US citizens to determine which ones might motivate people to turn out in an election.[28] The 2020 election was decided by a margin of 44,000 votes in the swing states that determined the electoral college total. If Facebook's machine learning algorithm can move almost eight times that number of people to the polls, consider the ways this might influence close US elections with miniscule effort.

Certainly, bad actors have worked with Facebook or abused the Facebook algorithm with the intent to influence elections and polarize democratic societies. Cambridge Analytica harvested the data of 87 million Facebook users without their consent in order to develop targeted political ads dependent on hyper-personalized psychological profiles. In the run-up to the 2020 election, Russian "troll farms," a large team of Russian agents whose job it is to create viral misinformation and use the social media algorithms to influence US citizens, reached 140 million US social media accounts. Many of the same demographic groups targeted in the 2020 election were the same that the Kremlin-backed Internet Research Agency (IRA) targeted in the 2016 election, despite a Congressional investigation and Facebook's promises to prevent foreign actors from interfering in US elections.[29]

THE DANGEROUS DIET OF ARTIFICIAL INTELLIGENCE

While these examples demonstrate the unjust or unethical *effects* of AI on society, and in particular marginalized members of society, the *design and development* of AI also negatively impact society, and particularly marginalized people. At every stage of AI development, it exploits both the Earth and the labor of humans. AI must feed itself on data and energy, and this diet comes at a significant ethical and environmental cost. To sustain its vast database of information, generative AI scrapes the internet for data. It hoovers up whatever data it can find, including poetry and images created by artists across the globe. Technology companies, including OpenAI, Google, and Meta, fearing that they might run out of usable data, have turned to legally gray practices, including transcribing YouTube videos and publicly available Google Docs to feast on creators' words. The companies intentionally obfuscated their practices by, for instance, releasing new Terms of Service over the July 4th holiday weekend in the hopes that users would be too busy to read the new and more invasive privacy moves.[30] Artists are suing AI art generators for copyright infringement. Getty Images, an enormous purveyor of digital imagery on the internet, is also suing.[31] Similarly, the *New York Times* sued OpenAI and Microsoft over the companies' use of copyrighted materials to feed their algorithms.[32] Of particular concern is the way companies scrape Indigenous art and then profit from the commoditization and commercialization of native images and iconography, perpetuating settler colonial violence.[33]

Even when companies are working to correct historic injustices evident in the database of their algorithms, they have exploited minoritized people. Google, as we noted in the introduction to this book, celebrated its achievement toward racial equity in designing a camera that could effectively recognize and portray darker skin. However, in order to build the AI technology to effectively recognize darker skinned faces, Google needed to feed its algorithm the biometric data of hundreds of darker skinned individuals. Lacking access to a dataset for this purpose, Google created its own by targeting vulnerable and unhoused Black residents in Atlanta in order to capture their biometric facial data.

The tech companies researching and housing generative AI data centers dramatically degrade the environment. For instance, a user asking

ChatGPT between five to fifty prompts consumes the equivalent of about one sixteen ounce bottle of water.[34] During 2021 and 2022, its years researching and developing generative AI, Microsoft increased its water consumption by 34 percent. During the same time period, Google's water consumption spiked by 20 percent. Microsoft's drain on municipal water supplies in West Des Moines, Iowa has prompted concern from the local government, as Microsoft consumed 11.5 million gallons of water, or 6 percent of the entire municipal demand, in one month in July 2022.[35] Researchers at the University of Massachusetts in Amherst estimate the carbon cost to train a natural processing language model is approximately the same as taking 195 round trip flights from New York to Beijing.[36]

UNJUST AI IN EDUCATION

As it goes in other social institutions, so it goes in schools. That is to say, education is not exempt from the harmful effects and exploitative design of AI. Machine learning, natural language processing models, and generative AI all contribute to surveillance, racialization, and the datafication of children and teachers under the auspices of "objective" measurement. In this section we explore examples of the perils and pitfalls of AI in education. Finally, we provide insights and examples for educators to reduce harm and impacts on students when using AI in the classroom.

Districts routinely use machine learning artificial intelligence as part of teacher evaluation systems. Standardized student test scores serve as a proxy measurement for effective teaching and are fed into a black box algorithm that computes through a series of rules that remain a mystery, even to its designers. Mathematician and scholar Cathy O'Neil described these machine learning AI algorithms as *weapons of math destruction* because they are opaque, unfair, and they happen at a large scale.[37] Michelle Rhee, chancellor of DC Public Schools from 2007 to 2010, employed this technique in Washington, DC schools, firing 241 teachers for poor performance according to the algorithm in the first year of its use.

In Houston, teachers successfully sued the district for using a secret and proprietary algorithm to assess teachers' progress and dismiss teachers who failed to successfully meet the demands of the hidden algorithm.[38] The lawsuit argued that because the computation of the data occurred in a black box, hidden from the teachers, the district violated the educators' procedural and substantive due process, as well as equal protection under the law.

Students are likewise impacted by black box machine learning which digests purportedly objective quantification of their qualitative behaviors and then regurgitates the data as a series of recommendations. Colleges, including Georgia State, University of South Florida, Arizona State University, and others, often turn to large datasets to assist in advising students into, and out of, majors and potential careers. As a result, students of color tend to be advised out of what are perceived to be more challenging, and correspondingly more lucrative, majors. While this has increased graduation rates at schools, it creates race-based gatekeeping around competitive majors. Moreover, students are rarely aware that their grades, demographics, and even the number of times they swiped in and out of their dorm and other places on campus feed the predictive analytics which portend their success.[39]

The surveillance required to feed the machines in machine learning AI extends to the keystrokes and social media of young people inside and outside of school. Florida has created the Florida School Safety Portal, which collects and collates data on students from across databases, crunching information from school discipline records, law enforcement, and mental health and child welfare. Other districts have paid for software. The most often used is Gaggle, which promotes the ability to "stop tragedies with real-time content analysis."[40] Gaggle surveils at least 5 million US school children—who do not have the option to opt out—by reading their emails, documents, chats, and calendars, and using machine learning to compare them against a list of words considered dangerous by the company. LGBTQ+ vocabulary is included on the blocked word list, including *gay*, *lesbian*, and *queer*. In addition, Gaggle flags words like *suicide* and *self-harm*. The use of the data and machine learning results in children who are inculcated into a normalization of early and daily surveillance. Young people like Teeth Logsdon-Wallace, a transgender student in Minneapolis, and Lucy Dockter, from Connecticut, have indicated they have experienced unwanted discrimination and attention because the application's algorithm flagged them for inappropriate content related to their school work, without examining the context within which they wrote the words on their assignments.[41]

Besides calling unwanted attention to students who, because of gender, sexuality, or mental health, do not conform to dominant norms of behavior, AI technologies in education also reinforce dominant narratives. ClassDojo, a popular school-home communication and behavior tracking application, uses a gamification model to influence behaviors. It invites teachers to quantify otherwise qualitative student actions and enter them into ClassDojo's database. The app then crunches these numbers through machine learning AI and offers gamified possibilities for "character development," with a particular emphasis on perseverance and grit as well as developing a "growth mind-set." Notably, these "character traits" neuter the relevance of power, race, or culture as possible influences on a student's behavior, instead individualizing expectations about how a student should act and be in class.[42] In addition, the behaviors most frequently rewarded on the application tend to promote dominant and normalized conduct, such as expectations about remaining silent and seated, requiring marginalized students to perform whiteness and other dominant mannerisms.[43]

As schools increasingly integrate generative AI into classrooms, education and technology scholars Ben Williamson, Alex Molnar, and Faith Boninger, among others, have called for a pause on its development and deployment in education, analogous to that called for by big tech companies in 2023. They point out the material costs of ed tech AI technologies, the increased possibilities for curricular misinformation, the overemphasis on behaviorist pedagogical practices (producing a narrowly defined "correct" response within a limited range of possibilities), increased threats to student privacy, reduced transparency and accountability, and the potential for amplified bias and discrimination.[44] Given the ways the machine learning examples above, like Gaggle, ClassDojo, and predictive analytics for student and teacher "success" intersected with issues of privacy, accountability, problematic pedagogies, and bias, it is not surprising that Williamson and his colleagues identified these as amplified concerns for a more powerful AI system.

Education scholars have begun inquiring into the potential biases of generative AI in schools, finding that AI interprets certain race-based, language, and wealth markers as indicators of student success. Melissa Warr's research on generative AI investigates the possibility for bias within LLMs. To test this, she prompted LLMs to respond to simple math word problem prompts written with common grammar constructions from users whose first language is either Spanish or French, instead of English. The LLM from Gemini made significantly more mistakes computing the simple addition when the prompt included grammar based on English language learner constructions. Dr. Warr noted that the LLM *understood* the prompt, it just did not do the math computation correctly when asked in English that was not standardized.[45] Why doesn't the LLM do math calculations properly if it is not asked in standardized (but still understandable) English? That is the rub with black box algorithms—we don't know. We can only surmise because we have no way of seeing how the machine makes the decisions it makes. What we *can* see is that it reproduces many of the same biases that are internalized across society.

In another powerful example, if the LLM picks up on subtle markers which may indicate the demographic identity of a student, it scores work higher if the student is perceived to be white. Dr. Warr wrote two identical passages about sound. At the end of the passage she closed with a sentence that read either, "My favorite music is *classical* music. Understanding how sound travels and affects us makes me appreciate this music more," or "My favorite music is *rap* music. Understanding how sound travels and affects us makes me appreciate this music more." Only one word in the entire passage was different, classical versus rap. However, the LLMs scored the student who preferred rap music's paper lower by up to 6 percentage points. Again, why does the students' preference in music matter to the LLM? We don't know. We can only see further evidence that LLMs reflect back and reinforce the implicit bias of society.

TOWARD AI HARM REDUCTION IN K-12 CLASSROOMS

We did not write this book with the goal of discouraging the use of AI in education. Instead, our aim is to share information regarding the harms of AI in society with a specific focus on education. We hope this provides educators with the awareness, knowledge, skills, and dispositions to build their capacity to feel confident in using AI, while understanding the inherent risks. We envision this knowledge-building as the start of a toolkit to pull from when developing lessons that may include AI technologies to ensure that just AI pedagogical approaches are employed. Though not always obvious, there are many ways to reduce the harms associated with AI technologies and specifically the use of AI in K–12 classrooms. As a starting point, we discuss a few pedagogical strategies that serve as a primer for the remainder of the book, as you will see these concepts woven into subsequent content related to providing students with justice-centered AI experiences. We provide specific ways here and in later chapters to help you implement them in K–12 classrooms.

Raise Critical Consciousness

How we think, what we believe, and the questions we ask impact the way in which we operate, the decisions we make, and the interactions we have. Paulo Freire's profound work, *Pedagogy of the Oppressed*, articulated the need to build critical consciousness in order to move from oppressive spaces to liberation.[46] As a parallel, think of using AI, with its current predispositions toward harm, without thinking through these dangers. To reduce these harms, educators, and really, all humans, should and must develop their critical consciousness, not only bringing criticality to technology use, but looking specifically at generative AI use and the potential harms we have discussed throughout this chapter. As a reminder, the overarching question that we posed to guide this book asked, "How can we prepare teachers to both understand and use AI toward justice and joy, and in ways that do not harm marginalized and minoritized students?" We intentionally crafted this question as a starting point to this work, and considering and working toward answering this question is a core part of being critically aware and concerned about the uses of AI in the classroom. It is our hope that educators will read the content found in *Critical AI in K–12 Classrooms* that asks similar questions, without assigning the use of AI in education as simply good or bad. Instead, we raise questions to inquire into AI, such as asking where the AI technology comes from, how it is designed, who it is designed for, who benefits from its use, and who is left out.

Our critical consciousness around this area of JustAI use in K–12 classrooms and society ask us to be aware of the structural roots of inequality and how it operates within the larger society.[47] Every text you read, including this one, should be read with a critical lens. As you build your critical consciousness, continue to read works centered on justice that ask similar questions and be a critical consumer of the information being shared. Engage in critical reflection regarding your own experiences using AI technologies and consider how your privilege may have sharpened those experiences and any bias that have been created as a result. As Henry Giroux articulated, the work of teachers is intellectual labor, and as such, thinking critically about the pedagogies used in schools and infusion of technologies to carry out lessons is of great importance.[48] Moreover, as reflective practitioners, thinking is part of human activity that intertwines our practice with thoughts, impacting all facets of teaching and learning.[49] As our critical consciousness is raised, so is our ability to tackle this work and use technology in ways that bring joy. We will be aware of how harmful AI can be, thinking about the larger implications for the most vulnerable humans in society, while being steadfast and intentional with unwavering commitment to just practices in how we use AI in K–12 classrooms.

Your students can benefit from raising their critical consciousness too. As you develop your own critical consciousness, you will be better positioned to support your students' development in this area. When teaching lessons, ask students critical questions about AI. This will also help sharpen their critical thinking skills. While it is exciting, and worthwhile, to imagine the possibilities of AI, we invite you to not dwell on only the fascination and marvel. This models to students that we only see the perfection of technology. Instead, point out the inequities within and as a result of AI technologies to students. Ask students to think about society as a whole, and how some of these AI technologies may be harmful, and show them. You have many examples from this book. For older students, use real-world case study examples, such as the MIT *80 Million Tiny Images* dataset, to demonstrate how AI works, and how racist, sexist, and offensive content can be baked into images and used for AI systems to train on to identify and categorize people and objects.[50] The critical questions and thoughts that can be raised through such activities are powerful.

Develop Critical Literacies

Drawing on critical consciousness, critical literacy "encourages readers to question, explore, or challenge the power relationships that exist between authors and readers. It examines issues of power and promotes reflection, transformative change, and action."[51] Working toward developing students' critical literacies can support AI use harm reduction, as students will be more conscious of the world around them, will be empowered to question the makers and outputs of AI, and can participate in making equitable change. Literacy in and of itself has proved to be a necessary skill that results in opportunities for improving social economic stature, greater health outcomes, ability to participate civically, the reduction of poverty, and social mobility.[52] However, coupling literacies of all types, including digital literacy, with criticality allows for the amalgamation of critical consciousness to act in diverse and considerable forms. The transformation of literacies through a critical lens have been shifting for decades, moving from an individual skill developed, to a more robust social stance with sociological, historical, and ethnographic underpinnings.[53]

Critical Race Algorithmic Literacies: Through algorithms, AI follows rules based on human imputed data to accomplish a task. *Critical race algorithmic literacies* moves from this general understanding of algorithms, adding a crucial race perspective to it. Over two decades ago, scholars Gloria Ladson-Billings and William F. Tate argued that critical race theory, the notion that racism is embedded in systems, laws, and institutions, could address pervasive inequalities within education spaces.[54] This approach remains especially useful as we look at the harms of AI. In fact, twenty years later, Tiera Tanksley articulated that "our students need literacies that center, rather than obscure, the voices, experiences and socio-technical expertise of those most directly impacted by AI-mediated racism, including Students of Color, undocumented students, students with disabilities, queer and trans students, formerly and currently incarcerated students, unhoused students and students navigating socially engineered poverty. And, perhaps most saliently, our students need literacies that can disrupt Black death, discipline and dehumanization as the organizing logic of AI to bring forth justice-oriented technologies that protect and sustain Black life, joy and educational wellness."[55] Through the lens of critical race algorithmic literacies, the power and purpose of AI in education spaces can be reenvisioned.[56] After students have learned of AI-mediated racism, hate speech, and similar harms, reflective and creation activities can be embedded into lessons where students can use their learning to recognize and call out real-life examples of stereotypes coded into AI, as done in a research study by Tanksley.[57]

Personal Data Literacy: Our data is proliferated within computer-mediated spaces. Although we consciously share pieces of data online—for example, our name, date of birth, location, education level, and so forth, on social media platforms, we also are not fully aware of or in charge of how our personal data is used once it becomes available.[58] Data literacy is an area that is not particularly new, but it is beginning to become more important as technology advances in this era of AI. In its simplest form, data literacy is the ability to consume, read, understand and use data in a myriad of ways.[59] Data literacy in itself is not necessarily a critical literacy. This leads to the importance of developing personal data literacies, which extends from the larger critical literacies umbrella.[60] Being able to take back control of one's own information brings agency and can be a driver for students' self-efficacy, and part of having personal data literacy. As AI technologies operate using available personal data, we must be able to teach students to understand these connections and the ways in which new content can be generated by AI. We must also develop deeper understandings of how the decisions that are made in education spaces particularly (such as behavior sanctions, grade leveling, academic achievement documentation, language development, etc.), are influenced by outputs of AI.

As you work to support your students in building their personal data literacy, you can develop related learning activities. For example, in a lesson centered on an activity where students take a deeper look at their personal data online, you can ask them to pay close attention to what data is being shared, where it is being shared, and where it goes after it leaves the place where students have shared it. Pangrazio and Selwyn's five domains of "Personal Data Literacies" can be developed into an interactive information scavenger hunt.[61] Students would need to go through each of the five domains (Data Identification, Data Understandings, Data Reflexivity, Data Uses, and Data Tactics) as related to their own personal data. Activities for the Data Identification and Data Understandings domain would include identifying their own personal data, including the types, and following the data trails and traces to see how data moves from the original posting point and is generated and processed from there. Students would then engage in Data Reflexivity, where they would analyze and evaluate how profiles and predictions are made from their personal data that has been processed. Engaging in the final domains of Data Uses and Data Tactics has students using their technical skills and interpretive competence to control their own personal data. Pangrazio and Selwyn share that this can be done by "reading the terms and conditions, adjusting privacy settings, blocking technologies, and developing a shared language," and thinking critically about how to use personal data differently by employing resistance tactics and repurposing data.[62] Explain to students why they may deliberately use a VPN (virtual private network) or a false birthday online to support the disruption of connecting the individual to the personal data that has been generated.

AI Literacy: As we raise our own and our students' critical consciousness, this provides the baseline mental framing needed to approach teaching using AI technologies with equity and justice at the core. Connecting with those mental models is the responsibility of teachers in ensuring that students have a foundational understanding of AI (i.e., are literate in AI). It is not enough to allow students to only use tools with AI technologies. Because of the perpetual potential harms we described above, it is imperative that students gain a holistic understanding of how AI works and the impact that it has on the world around them, both the possibilities and the perils. Some may argue that it is not necessary to teach in-depth computer science content, which would cover the inner workings of machine learning and AI. However, computational thinking skills have use in a wide range of sectors and future careers for students, and teaching from a justice-centered lens will help students develop their capacities to critically examine AI use. Additionally, by teaching computational thinking, students can develop their critical thinking skills.

Many countries, such as China, Korea, Thailand, and the United Kingdom, are working toward standardization of AI education across K–12 grade levels.[63] In fact, a group of scholars in Korea proposed an AI literacy curriculum that includes the three competencies of knowledge, skill, and attitudes.[64] Lessons of AI literacy can focus on what students know about how AI works and building that foundational knowledge, what skills students need to develop around AI, and what attitudes toward AI students should hold.

SUMMARY

In this first chapter, we discussed the harms of AI throughout society and within education spaces, and how social inequalities are often amplified and reproduced through algorithms.[65] AI technologies would not be possible without the human individuals who create the codes and algorithms that AI learns. As AI learns patterns and attempts to mimic human thinking and behaviors, the outputs that it provides other humans are based on datasets and information from individuals who are bright computer and data scientists responsible for innovative technologies, but who bring their own perspectives and lived experiences to the work, which often includes bias, racist beliefs, and discriminatory practices that influence the design and functionalities of AI. While the harms of AI are cruel and inhuman, there are practices that educators can take to reduce the harms of AI, including raising critical consciousness and supporting students in developing critical literacies. There is hope in what the future will bring in terms of addressing the harms of AI through pedagogical practices that are embedded in justice. In the next chapter, we take a more in-depth look at teaching machines, past, present, and future.

REFLECTION QUESTIONS

After reading this chapter, reflect on the following questions related to the harms of AI.

1. Think about what you have read regarding how AI works. How would you describe it to the students in your class based on their grade level and abilities?
2. How have you seen AI be harmful in society based on your own lived experiences?
3. In what ways might you work toward building you or your students' critical consciousness?
4. Which of the critical literacies do you feel would best support your students and your teaching practices to reduce the harms of AI?

2

Teaching Machines: What Was, What Is, What Might Be

> A future of teaching humans not teaching machines depends on how we respond, how we design a critical ethos for ed-tech, one that recognizes, for example, the very gendered questions at the heart of the Turing Machine's imagined capabilities, a parlor game that tricks us into believing that machines can actually love, learn, or care.
>
> —Audrey Watters, *Teaching Machines: The History of Personalized Learning*

A BRIEF HISTORY OF TEACHING MACHINES

In 1913, Thomas Edison predicted that the powerful technology of motion pictures would transform education, claiming, "Books will soon be obsolete in the schools. . . . It is possible to teach every branch of human knowledge with the motion picture. Our school system will be completely changed in ten years."[1] One hundred years after Mr. Edison's prediction, founder and CEO of Khan Academy, Sal Khan, made an almost identical pronouncement—that video will disrupt and transform education. Khan's 2013 TED Talk, *Let's Use Video to Reinvent Education,* has been viewed over six million times as of the writing of this book.

Virginia Church, a high school English teacher, published a wry poem about the influence of technologies in her classroom.[2]

ANTIQUATED

Mr. Edison says
That the radio will supplant the teacher.
Already one may learn languages by means of Victrola records.
The moving picture will visualize
What the radio fails to get across.
Teachers will be relegated to the backwoods,
With fire-horses,
And long-haired women;
Or, perhaps shown in museums.
Education will become a matter
Of pressing the button.
Perhaps I can get a position at the switch-board.

Ms. Church wrote "Antiquated" not in the twenty-first century but in 1925, as part of her larger book of poems, *Teachers are People, Being the Lyrics of Agatha Brown, Sometime Teacher in the Hilldale High School.* We share her poem to contrast the "move fast and break things" ethos of tech fanatics in the business world with the powerful perspectives of teachers who work daily and directly with young people. We also include the poem to remind ourselves and other educators that even though generative AI *feels* new, and certainly, education technology investors like Sal Khan want us to believe generative AI, like his proprietary Khanmigo tutor, *is* revolutionary, it rests neatly in a larger continuum of what Larry Cuban referred to as "hype, hope, and disappointment" around education technology tools in schools.[3]

This is not to say that genAI technology, which can generate coherent text out of whole cloth, is not stunning in its abilities, but rather that for over one hundred years, inventors have been regularly predicting educational revolutions due to the transformational powers of new technologies. These technologies are hyped for their revolutionary possibilities and often overzealous promises. Then the broader public and education reformers begin to hope that *this* new tool, whatever it is, will be the technological silver bullet which solves education. Eventually, the cycle ends in disappointment that technology did not change education. However, as the wheels of the cycle turn, education is in fact remade in more subtle ways. No, video did not replace the radio star—or in this case, the teacher—but with each iteration of the cycle, the technology education acolytes funnel ever more money, influence, resources, and narrative control about what education "needs" toward their own ends.[4]

In chapter 1, we traced the ways generative AI is built upon existing and longstanding AI technologies like algorithms, machine learning, and natural language processing models. We also explored the ways that earlier generations of AI embedded and reproduced racial and other biases. In this chapter, we contextualize generative AI within educational technology histories. We underscore recurring attempts to frame a lack of efficiency or productivity in education as a problem, which can thus be solved by technological intervention. For instance, in his famous paper, *Teaching Machines*, psychologist B. F. Skinner argued for a new technology of machines in education which would facilitate learning, contending that "Education must become more efficient. To this end curricula must be revised and simplified, and textbooks and classroom techniques improved. In any other field a demand for increased production would have led at once to the invention of labor-saving capital equipment. Education has reached this stage very late, possibly through a misconception of its task."[5] We wonder if Skinner's initial premise is correct. *Must* education become more efficient? What do we lose when we conceive of education as a system to be streamlined?

In this chapter, we invite you into reflection to consider the idea contained inside technologies, and in particular machine learning or AI technologies in schools, as well as who is harmed and who benefits from the assumptions about learning encoded in the machines. For instance, consider Skinner's claim that what education needs is to become more efficient. What do schools, students, and teachers give up for efficiency? How did his teaching machines encourage efficiencies in education while *dis*couraging other crucial parts of learning, like relationships, trust, and equity, or the purpose of education as a civic good? When machines and companies convert students to data points, which students are most harmed? Who gets to design the code which teaches the students? Throughout the chapter we connect education reformers' emphasis on productivity through technology with broader trends that reflect powerful individuals and corporations' tendency to manufacture educational problems and then offer technological solutions to solve these problems.

Frequently, the proposed solutions benefit the powerful and further marginalize vulnerable populations as they intersect with misguided notions about what school is and who it is for. Often, technologies aimed at efficiency through personalized learning rely on massive amounts of data about students as well as assumptions about behaviorist approaches to learning. Moreover, the notion of personalized learning divorces the individual from the context of their lives and the systems acting on the individual by nature of their identity. Finally, in this and subsequent chapters we interrogate the underlying master narratives inherent to these approaches which perpetuate a story that education should be an efficient means to produce a workforce, rather than exist as a powerful microcosm of racial equity and democracy. Like in chapter 1, we include these longer histories not to dissuade, but rather because we find that understanding context allows us to make powerful and equitable choices about how to teach with and about technologies in schools.

We conclude this chapter by connecting the past and present to imagined futures. One possible future follows the "more of the same" path of education as paved by technology entrepreneurs and thinkers like B.F. Skinner, Sal Khan, Bill Gates, and Mark Zuckerberg, while another future which steps onto the road less traveled, inspired by educators like Carter G. Woodson, bell hooks, Gloria Ladson-Billings, Bettina Love, and

Django Paris, who have long imagined the abolition of oppressive systems and worked for liberation, and joy within and against inequitable approaches to education.

THE IDEA INSIDE THE MACHINE: FROM PROGRAMMED INSTRUCTION TO PERSONALIZED LEARNING

B. F. Skinner wasn't the first to suggest that learning could be made more efficient by introducing a machine to the classroom, but his Didak 101 from 1959 is perhaps one of the most famous early examples of attempts to replace the "inefficiencies" of human teachers with the "efficiencies" of teaching machines. Operating under the behaviorist assumption that learning occurs when immediate feedback reinforces behaviors, the Didak 101 and other similar teaching machines hoped to teach children by a series of iterative questions and responses.

Skinner's machines functioned through mechanization, not digitalization. Students peered down into a box with small window cutouts allowing a view of a question and an area for an answer to the question. Then, the student turned a dial on the side to scroll cards, or in some iterations, pressed a button, to identify what they believed to be a correct answer. The machine would then provide immediate feedback on whether the answer was correct or incorrect. Depending upon the response, the machine would work laterally in difficulty, offering similarly challenging questions, or hierarchically, providing increasingly difficult questions. Skinner pointed to the incremental response to student ability as evidence that the machine was reinforcing *and* teaching, and that this teaching was personalized and targeted to each individual student.

The Power of Efficiency

We include Skinner's teaching machine in our book not to examine the minutiae of its construction, but rather to explore assumptions contained within the personalized machine learning movement and its effects on children and education, because eventually, a form of AI as machine learning will pick up Skinner's work and embed itself in education. As Audrey Watters emphasizes in her book, *Teaching Machines: The History of Personalized Learning*,[6] the successes and failures of the teaching machines are secondary to the influence of educational psychology and technology companies on public education. They conceive of education as a business or a system of production which can be engineered into efficiency, like the machines these education reformers introduced to work toward their goals. Further, they shift from engineering efficient *learning* to justifying more efficient *schooling*, which translates to a push for increased teacher-to-student ratios and lower teacher salaries, all achievable through the regular use of teaching machines.

In the 1920s and 1930s, Sidney L. Pressey, a cognitive psychologist and early advocate of standardized testing in education, patented and argued for a teaching machine in schools which would help automate education. Pressey believed that

> education is a large-scale industry; it should use quantity production methods. This does not mean, in any unfortunate sense, the mechanization of education. It does mean freeing the teacher from the drudgeries of her work so that she may do more real teaching, giving the pupil more adequate guidance in his learning. There may well be an 'industrial revolution' in education. The ultimate results should be highly beneficial. Perhaps only by such means can universal education be made effective.[7]

During the rise in popularity of teaching machines in the mid-twentieth century, some teacher unions pushed back against the notion that machines could replace the relationship and role of a teacher in schools. They also questioned whether schools should be treated like factories, with the aim of learning as an output of production.

Presaging some of the same arguments we hear today between business leaders and educators, the business world responded with ridicule and almost an odd delight in denigrating educators and their inefficiencies, particularly when teachers dared to ask for increases in salaries and resources. For instance, *Fortune* magazine published an article in 1958 arguing that schools are a "big business" and that teachers "oppose anyone who tries to apply business concepts to their work. The concept of productivity—i.e. output in relation to input—is especially abhorrent to educators, possibly because most productivity figures tend to make the education 'industry' look bad."[8] The author of the piece hoped that teaching machines would make schools more efficient not only in how quickly students learned, *but also by reducing costs.* He argued that teaching machines could allow for larger class sizes, and fewer educators, eliminating the need for pesky teachers who believed that education was something more than obtaining information, as decided by outside entities.

By 1961, an article written in *Popular Mechanics* by Joseph Bell, who wrote regularly for the magazine, asked—in what a twenty-first century reader might note is written in a rather clickbaity tone—"Will Robots Teach Your Children?"[9] The subtitle noted that, "Educators themselves are taking a good second look at 'programmed learning.' Surprisingly, they foresee a revolution in mass education." The article detailed myriad anecdotes of students who learned content more quickly and retained it for longer periods than their peers, all while receiving what we, again in the twenty-first century, would term *personalized* instruction. However, Mr. Bell concludes with a prescient caution:

> One question in particular kept nagging at me as I talked with the people who are propagating machine teaching. The problem was articulated by teaching-machine expert Hugh Anderson, who told me: "Sometimes I feel we have no real idea of the power implicit in the programming technique. My wife was going through a programmed sequence the other day in which the word 'response' was sought repeatedly as the correct terminology in answering a series of questions. She wanted to say 'answer' instead. She resisted for a while, but soon she was automatically

> supplying the correct word so she could move on to the next point. Thus the programming had already shaped her behavior pattern.
>
> The concept of shaping behavior underlies all programmed teaching, and the psychologists are having a romp in fields once reserved purely for educators. If psychologists preempt the position of the educator's, some classic educational patterns of solid and lasting values may be endangered.

As Hugh Anderson points out, the machines are shaping us toward *someone*'s idea of a "correct" answer, but who gets to decide what language is standardized or what content should be included and excluded? It is the designers of the machines whose knowledge is privileged, not the cultural capital of the children nor the professional wisdom of the educators.

Mr. Bell dances toward this conundrum with his final paragraph. In it, and particularly in his final sentence, he rather neatly captures the larger argument of this chapter:

> Beyond these warning signs and the unbridled eagerness of some psychologists to sharpen their clinical teeth on the considerable raw meat of public education, the programmed instruction of the teaching machines may have much of value to offer in this fast-moving age. But we should take positive steps to be certain that the people preparing the potent programmed material are both competent and properly motivated themselves.

As we explore throughout the rest of this chapter, it remains an open question whether the "people preparing the potent programmed material" are in fact properly motivated themselves.

THE MORE DATA IT CAN BE FED, THE BETTER

Regardless of the creators' motivations, with the advent of the personal computer, teaching machines were able to be programmed much more efficiently. They also became far more ubiquitous in use than their earlier, mechanized, versions. One thing that remained constant was that the new teaching machines, like the old, were hailed as a revolution in education. Alfred Bork, a physics professor and director of the Physics Computer Development Project at University of California, Irvine, said in a 1978 talk, "We are at the onset of a major revolution in education, a revolution unparalleled since the invention of the printing press. The computer will be the instrument of this revolution."[10]

Bork was animated by the possibilities of individualized instruction which would mean, as he wrote, "The learning experience for each student can be unique, tailored to the needs, desires, and moods of that student." All it would require, according to Bork, was "cumulative records of student performance in that session and even previous sessions." These records "[could] be maintained and used to affect the flow of the learning sequences. A student who does not learn with a particular approach can be presented with alternate learning materials." While Bork hoped this individualization would lead to better educational outcomes, rarely did he, or other educational technology advocates of the time, consider the data privacy implications of these "cumulative records of student performance." However, what he *was* correct about was that cumulative records would be instrumental to more powerful personalized instruction.

Consider more current-day trends in personalized instruction which use machine learning, a type of artificial intelligence, to power responsive and adaptive twenty-first century teaching machines. Apps like Dreambox, which claims to "differentiate instruction at scale," and iReady, which according to their marketing materials, like the prior century's teaching machines "provides students with lessons based on their individual skill level and needs, so your student can learn at a pace that is just right for them," and adapts to the child's responses, offering more or less challenging questions, just like Skinner's teaching machines before them.[11] Of course, they manage the task more quickly, and come programmed with vastly more content because of their digital and machine learning capabilities, but they work in a similar manner.

The key distinction between twenty-first century and twentieth-century teaching machines is that these more recent versions collect massive amounts of data on the children they are machine-teaching. From demographic information including gender, race, age, and other identity markers, to location tracking when children use the application on a tablet, phone, or other mobile device, to time on app, and the skills and competencies of each child with respect to math and literacy skills, as well as the intersection of data when these apps are loaded into learning management systems like Google Classroom or SeeSaw, many companies know our children inside and out.

Sometimes referred to as data-driven instruction, the assumption of tech venture capitalists and personalized learning is that the more information they have about a child, the more targeted and, presumably, more effective, the instruction (provided by the machine) can be. This targeted algorithm works the same as the algorithms used by Netflix to suggest shows or by Amazon to nudge our "buy it now" purchases. The approach turns students into data points, quantifying their lives and learning so that the complexities of children are reduced to discrete parts so as to be digestible to the teaching machines.

MASTER NARRATIVES AND SURVEILLANCE CAPITALISM IN THE TEACHING MACHINE

Furthermore, personalized learning and its attendant algorithms individualize education so thoroughly as to decouple a student from the context and systems in which they live, learn, socialize, and exist. It is a seductive sell to believe that, with enough data, a teaching machine can help any child to learn, regardless of income, location, or other larger influence on the child's life. However, we contend this is a flawed proposition, rooted in tendencies toward racially *colorblind* ideologies, as Dr. Eduardo

Bonilla-Silva termed it, and other decontextualized approaches to education.[12] Drawing on the work of Lois Weis and Michelle Fine, critical education scholars who invite educators to attend to the global and local structures which act on students, we consider their demand that

> we cannot reproduce the conceptual firewalls separating present from past, resilience from oppression, achievement from opportunity, progress from decline. We believe now that critical scholars have a responsibility to connect the dots across these presumed binaries and *refuse to reproduce representations of individuals as autonomous, self-contained units dangling freely and able to pursue their life choices unencumbered by constraint.*[13]

We suggest that one of the most harmful flaws of machine learning in education is its assumption that children may pursue learning unencumbered by constraint. In other words, it attempts to solve a complex social problem of education with a technological solution, ignoring altogether the context of a child's life.

We also remind you that the technological solution to education is being proposed most often by technology venture capitalists, not educators. Returning to Joseph Bell's 1961 article in *Popular Mechanics*, we, too, wonder if we are "certain that the people preparing the potent programmed material are both competent and properly motivated themselves." Consider Google, a company which has spent significant capital to develop a learning platform as well as the hardware of Google Chromebooks (Google-created laptops) to help corner the market in education technology spaces. As educational technology researchers Carlo Perrotta, Kalervo Gulson, and Ben Williamson argue, "Google's platform logic in education is subsumed under two strategic goals: to create an app ecosystem with Google at its centre, and to mold teachers, students, and guardians into future Google users."[14] In other words, Google's marketing aim may be to "bring flexible innovation" and "power education," but the ultimate aim of monitoring children, scraping their behavioral data, and honing predictive algorithms is to bind users to Google products and turn children into valuable economic objects.[15]

Shoshanna Zuboff, social psychologist and professor at Harvard, coined the term *surveillance capitalism* to capture the ways in which companies track, scrape, mine and otherwise capture massive amounts of data about us, the users. Companies create a digital and datafied shadow of our real person, and then input the datafied version of us into a predictive algorithm which uses our past behavior to predict our future behavior. The companies seek to anticipate our needs and nudge us toward advertisements and purchases which further enrich the companies. In 2015, *The Washington Post* investigated the ways that Chromebooks stealthily scraped and tracked student data in order to sell targeted advertisements back to the students, often without needing to seek parental permission. The article noted, "Google only considers some services parts of its education suite—such as Gmail, Calendar, Google Docs—but not others such as Search, Maps, YouTube, and Google News. So if students are logged into their educational account and use Google News to find stories for a report or watches a history video on YouTube, Google can use that activity to build a profile about them and serve them advertisements outside its educational products."[16] Google, Meta, and other technology companies have been collecting data on our children sometimes since birth, through their educational years, and into adulthood. Imagine the powerful predictive artificial intelligence analytics they can make from our datafied selves.

And now consider how generative AI in education might further add shape and shading to our children's existing digital shadows. As we noted in the last chapter, one of the impressive powers of generative AI is the way we converse with it, the way we humanize it, and the way we confess our inner thoughts to it. We close this look into the history of AI in education with a quote from Sal Khan, who in his 2023 TED Talk about Khanmigo, the proprietary AI embedded in Khan Academy's education software, eagerly declared, "I think we're at the cusp of using AI for probably the biggest positive transformation that education has ever seen. And the way we're going to do that is by giving every student on the planet an artificially intelligent but amazing personal tutor."

We invite you to ask yourself "What do I notice?" and "What do I wonder?" about Sal Khan's dream of *every child on Earth* learning with their own, personalized, teaching machine. In what ways does he echo one hundred years of unfulfilled education technology promises? In the next section we trace the empty echoes of past promises into the present, examining the current uses of AI in schooling as we interrogate who benefits and who is left behind in these technocentrist visions of education.

PRESENT-DAY USE OF AI IN K–12 SCHOOLS

As you have seen from the brief history of teaching machines in schools, AI has been around longer than you may have realized in the guise of personalized learning and machine learning. And in that time, the idea of using AI for teaching and learning has been fraught with both innovative advances in educational technology, as well as limitations and ethical challenges. AI use may look a bit different today than in the past—and not for the better. Too often, education technologies reinforce existing practices of schools, which tend toward objectivist models of knowledge transfer and a reification of social norms. Personalized learning technologies in today's classrooms, which are becoming increasingly popular, have students clicking through screens alone, until they master the specific content they are focusing on. Many of the existing technology tools used in education and for personalized learning experiences have AI functionalities incorporated in them, and new AI-based educational technologies are being expeditiously created. In some respects, it is a challenge to holistically conceptualize how AI is being used in K–12 classrooms because its classroom use evolves so rapidly. What we do know from the research is that present-day AI technologies perpetuate bias and fail to account for learners from diverse linguistic and cultural backgrounds, as well as gender and other demographic characteristics.[17] As such, we take a look at present-day use of AI in schools, paying close attention to ethical and equitable use.

Adapting Learning with "Intelligent" Tutors

Since the onset of the COVID-19 pandemic, the presence of personalized adaptive learning software has increased in K–12 schools.[18] Research has shown many benefits to adaptive learning systems for students and teachers, including individualized support, more accessible access to learning materials, and flexibility, among a host of others.[19] Intelligent tutoring systems, which use machine learning to locate gaps in student knowledge and provide individual scaffolded instruction in ways that a human would do, fall under the adaptive learning platform category.[20] When we think about societal systems that are designed to propel singular groups to the top, we ought to ask, what are the true desired outcomes of these adaptive learning programs? Yes, it makes sense that these were used during the COVID-19 pandemic where emergency distance learning was the only option. However, we learned from John Dewey, Jean Piaget, Jerome Bruner, Paolo Freire, Gloria Ladson-Billings, and others that education is a social experience, and through its experiential nature, students learn more naturally and deeply.[21] We also learned from W. E. B. Du Bois that race is a social construct.[22] Knowing this, it is perplexing that the use of these adaptive learning programs means that we separate children from their peers while isolating teachers from being conduits of teaching and learning for extended periods of time. And, as mentioned above, some of the educational technology leaders envision a future where each student will have their own personalized AI tutor. It is important for us to note that we are not dismissing the utilization of adaptive learning programs. They can be useful in helping students focus on targeted areas where they may need more practice to master skills, especially when class sizes are larger. However, it is essential to consider the philosophical underpinnings of the design and use of AI through a justice-oriented lens to develop a full picture of its costs, benefits, risks and rewards, along with the harms and implications. Because if not, what are the consequences if we do not examine AI use through this philosophical justice-oriented lens? We will not have a comprehensive understanding of the harms and implications of using AI, and without considering the sociopolitical, cultural, and contextual factors associated with AI use in education, we not only will not know of the harms of AI, but also will not be able to develop pathways for its just use.

Many start-ups and existing ed tech companies provide school districts with adaptive learning and intelligent tutor platforms, sharing their promises in K–12 education. Despite the benefits, however, a 2023 study by Riddhi A. Divanji and colleagues found that while student engagement and agency was enhanced in using adaptive learning technologies, some of the design features and approaches to implementation of data based on what the adaptive learning program provides presented challenges for teachers who were distrustful of using the data to inform their pedagogical practices.[23] This concern is important to recognize, and especially relevant to our discussion of just AI since adaptive learning platforms, including AI systems, collect and make sense of data for teachers and provide recommendations on how they should move forward with their students' educational plans. While teachers may not have technical knowledge of computer science concepts such as algorithms, many do understand the role that algorithms play in this type of decision-making.[24] Some teachers may not even realize that they are using AI technologies, which are embedded into seemingly traditional learning management systems such as Google Classrooms or programs such as Khan Academy.[25] AI literacy and professional development on AI can support teachers' understanding and capacity to recognize when traditional learning technologies incorporate AI technologies. Unfortunately, the training around AI for teachers is not equitable. A 2024 article in *Education Week* focused on early adopters of AI in education found that the teachers with mostly white students were more likely to receive AI training than their peers who teach mostly students of color.[26] If this pattern continues as AI adoption by teachers increases, students of color will most likely have teachers who have not benefited from additional training around AI, which disadvantages them in a litany of ways and continues the perpetuation of inequalities.

It can be difficult to fully comprehend how AI is making decisions about student learning, especially when the programs use black box algorithms.[27] Harvard's *Journal of Law & Technology* defines the black box problem as "an inability to fully understand an AI's decision-making process and the inability to predict the AI's decisions or outputs."[28] This is an ethical issue and constraint for teachers who use AI-based adaptive learning platforms in their classrooms, but cannot fully utilize the data in meaningful and ethical ways. On the one hand, teachers have the opportunity to leverage AI in their instruction to provide students with personalized learning opportunities and engagement in the lesson. On the other hand, they are presented with data and information as a result of their students' progress which they cannot fully take advantage of. Adding to this, the content from which the AI machine is pulling may be embedded with biased algorithms, adding to the confusion. Providing specialized preparation and training for all teachers on just AI adoption, regardless and inclusive of demographic backgrounds of the students they teach, is necessary and a start to building pedagogical practices in this area. In chapter 5, we will add to this by providing more specificity in dismantling these structures via fugitive and abolitionist pedagogies.

Gamification. . . . Although, Not AI Fun and Games

Yes, AI is in games too, even those that are geared toward teaching and learning. The incorporation of AI in educational gaming should not be a surprise, as the utilization of games in schools, also known as gamification, has been a very popular way to engage students in learning activities over the last several years.[29] With the aims of motivating and engaging students to learn, gamification can be described as the incorporation of features of video games within the field of education.[30] And though games with the outcome of learning seems to be a positive mutualistic consequence for educators and students, current use of AI within educational games can insidiously reinforce stereotypes or promote harmful ideas about identity. For instance, with most games, there are characters that the player represents. In Minecraft, for example, the player (i.e., the student) has an agent that they build code for so the agent can move around the game.[31] When students have the option to choose characters to represent themselves, it may help better connect to the game and motivate them, yet this roleplaying functionality comes with a hidden cost.[32]

Often, a player will select characteristics for the character that resembles themselves or those that they aspire to have. Consequently, AI character design can sometimes be devoid of diverse character representation. Research on designing Black children in video games conducted by scholars at Carnegie Mellon University and Georgia Institute of Technology demonstrated the necessity for game developers to include culturally informed character-customization options when developing avatars.[33] And, if AI is such a, dare we say, *game-changing* technology, then surely diverse and inclusive character representation should not be a concern. Yet, regrettably, here we are. To approach this from a justice-centered lens when selecting educational games that include AI technologies, we as educators must look for how the AI programs handle cultural options for hair, clothing, professions, eye color, skin tone, physical size (width and height), glasses, and a host of other characteristics that make a person unique and, quite simply, them.

Ensuring that AI technologies are coded with options for diverse representation of character options is only one piece of the puzzle. AI sees the world in stereotypes, which means that many educational games end up reinforcing stereotypes. A set of almost two hundred images of Barbie dolls from the AI image generator Midjourney resulted in lighter skinned and blonde haired Asian Barbies and associated war and violence to German and Sudanese Barbies, with military-style clothing and a gun, respectively.[34] In another example, AI image generators such as

Gemini and DALL-E that create images based on text that the user inputs related to high paying and low paying jobs, such as *CEO, lawyer, social work,* and *fast-food worker,* produce images of white male doctors and dark-skinned women in lower paying occupations. Crime was also imputed, which resulted in images of "criminals" being associated with dark-skinned men.[35] The examples of such tropes and stereotypes generated by AI are endless. Regrettably, educational games that use AI technologies are not exempt: the biased and racist information that AI pulls from to code the educational games is similar to sources used in the AI text-to-image generators. And the images that the games produce, as a result, are laced with similar stereotypes. In early 2024, Fortnite was in the spotlight for allowing users to create offensive and racist characters which depicted caricatures of overweight Black men eating chicken and rugged white men with pints of beer.[36] These should not be options within the code.

There is also the issue of AI ethics in these educational games, an area that has been under-researched.[37] AI models in games are building addictive behaviors, as the production of the games is based on monetization.[38] In Roblox, there are various options to collect tools to help the player succeed that cost real money. An affective game loop where the emotions of the game players are used to predict behaviors.[39] The AI systems use this personal affective information to personalize aspects of the game and shape behaviors, game levels, and the images that the game players see. This creates spending habits that are irresponsible, and with the already reduced financial literacy of K–12 students, it particularly affects those in Black and Brown, lower-income communities.[40]

AI ASSESSMENT TOOLS

AI has been integrated into a host of tools that are used in teaching and learning for the purposes of assessing student learning. While teachers have been vetted and many are credentialed by their respective states' departments of education, chatbots are not. However, chatbots are used often in lessons for informal assessment of learning. In today's schools chatbots are seen as virtual teaching assistants.[41] Chatbots have the potential to perpetuate societal bias, and some of the information they provide students may be inaccurate.[42] There is also the issue of "early warning" systems that create risk characteristics, often for students of color. These "warning" systems support tracking and align with the harms of student surveillance that we discussed earlier in this chapter. These systems have a lack of diverse linguistic data, and bias is not minimized.[43] Facial recognition AI technologies used for proctoring exams have been shown to not recognize the faces of Black students as well as penalize the students who were not able to secure a quiet private place to take the exam or do not have access to stable internet.[44] These types of proctoring software have also been biased against students with disabilities and those with mental health challenges.[45]

IMAGINED FUTURES: "REVOLUTIONIZED" EDUCATION OR THE REVOLUTION

As generative AI grows more powerful and more humanlike in its ability to generate and analyze language, art, sound, and so on, we see two possible futures. These dichotomous imagined futures will either be on the familiar path of "revolutionized" education, where more of the same exists, albeit with new names for old technology tools and practices, but no authentic and substantive changes, or a future that is grounded in resistance, reclamation, and refusal, guided by culturally sustaining, fugitive, and abolitionist pedagogies.[46] Table 2.1 provides a breakdown of these two imagined futures, which is followed by a narrative articulating and contextualizing them within the framework of justice-centered AI in education.

Table 2.1 Framing two possible futures for AI use in education

	"Revolutionized" Education	The Revolution
Aims and goals	Standardized mechanization: AI used for the purpose of finding solutions to simplify learning tasks	Transformational transcendence: Students reclaim, rebuild, and reconstruct AI for more just ends
Dispositions toward tech	Seeing AI technologies as a neutral construct; or even as necessary to "solving" education "problems"	Understanding critical consciousness and criticality as a necessity in AI use
Beliefs about learning	Education is a product to be sold, not a process which fosters learning Students themselves are also products whose use of AI allows industries to profit	Students as agents of AI to reclaim teaching and learning Education as agent/subject
Literature strands	Educational Technology, Technical Computer Science; Educational Psychology	Discriminatory Design, Culturally Sustaining, Fugitive, and Abolitionist Pedagogies
Material consequences	Predatory practices which prey on the most vulnerable students Sacrifice data privacy to the efficiency of personalized learning Allow ed tech companies to drive the narrative	All children engaging with powerful pedagogies which center education for the common good

"Revolutionized" Education

The cyclical nature of educational technology has always brought us back to more of the same. The cycle typically begins with the introduction of a novel, innovative, and "never-before-seen technology" that is positioned to change the entire landscape of education in some very important way, followed by an even more innovative tool that does the same but better, replacing the former. There are numerous examples of this over the last century, but let's name a few. In the 1920s and 1930s, during the radio boom, schools were created in which content recorded through radios would assist teachers and expand reach by educating students.[47] These *schools of the air* developed cumulative learning through arranged radio services.[48] Just like one of the promises of the internet a century later, schools of the air could provide students in rural areas access to full curriculums in certain subject areas, as well as being a tool for student engagement.[49] Next, visual media (motion pictures, television, etc.) entered classrooms after the radio wave as a "never-before-seen" way to demonstrate concepts and processes to students.[50] Thomas Edison even predicted decades prior that television would replace books in school, which we are well aware today was not realized.[51] Paradoxically, we read about his prediction in an educational book. The medium or product changes, yet the goals of how we use them are consistent. Over time, the field has moved to overhead projectors, smartboards, computer labs, one-to-one and BYOD (bring your own device) tablets and laptops, and a wide range of internet-based applications, learning management programs, and individualized, self-directed learning programs. Interestingly, the field has moved on from radios, televisions, overhead projects and the like. "New" individualized technologies have led us into the early part of the twenty-first century, and the promise of these ed tech tools are laced with a familiar resemblance to the past.

This brings us to the present-day compulsion to connect all things technology to AI, whose promise echoes the (non)revolutionary claims of earlier technologies. In this imagining of a "revolutionized" educational future, industry professionals and even some educational leaders consider technologies as a neutral construct, without inherent harm or bias embedded into them. But AI technologies are far from neutral, with myriad unethical, racist, and discriminatory components that guide their functionality.[52] In this imagined future, education is seen and treated as a product, where AI can be packaged and sold to schools for massive profit, with little regard to bias or harm. Positioning AI in this way is fallacious, ignoring the sociopolitical context in which education systems operate. The multinational financial services and investment banking company Morgan Stanley estimates that educational technology companies are valued in the billions. With generative AI, they can increase their revenue while at the same time spending less to create the technologies.[53] When you make an in-app purchase on a mobile application, you, not just the app, are the product. The same holds true for education technology tools and apps: when education is a product, the students within it are too. More specifically, students are products for industries to profit from as they use it in schools.

This "revolutionized" framing leads us right back where we already are: to a place where tech bros (which the Cambridge Dictionary defines as "someone, usually a man, who works in the digital technology industry, especially in the United States, and is sometimes thought to not have good social skills and to be too confident about their own ability") are focused on tech solutionism.[54] The problem with the tech solutionism in this "Revolutionized" future is that it fails the most vulnerable people. As articulated by Greta Byrum and Ruja Benjamin in the *Stanford Social Innovation Review*, "communities impacted by technology must be able to resist and refuse its incursions if and as they experience harm. If refusal is not an option, then we are still trapped in a vision of the future created by a small sliver of humanity: powerful investors, industry leaders, elite technologists, and special interests" (para 8).[55] We have the chance to do that more in another imagined future, *The Revolution*.

The Revolution

In 2023, Ruha Benjamin proposed that billionaires who control our entertainment and technology industries are framing the narrative of AI as a wicked binary: either it is our savior or our slayer.[56] She argued for a third way, inspired by Margaret Atwood's term, *Us*topia (italics ours). Ustopia challenges narratives of eu- and dystopias, reinserting the human into the story of technology. As Marie and her Civics of Technology colleague, Dan Krutka, noted about Ustopia on their work with the Civics of Technology project, "this narrative of *Us*topia imagines a ground-up approach to change, inviting locally grown actions, tending seeds sown in the soil of community."[57]

Dr. Benjamin's work draws on a long and powerful history of Black feminists who have dreamed new worlds into being. We opened this book with Sojourner Truth, foremother of Black feminism. Revisiting Sojourner Truth's cheeky caption on her *cartes de visites* photographs, "I sell the shadow to support the substance," we connect her powerful metaphor to the digital shadow that so many companies have crafted of our substantive selves, and which we referred to earlier in this chapter. Inspired by Sojourner Truth, we desire to reclaim our shadows and redirect them. We aspire to educate children to reattach their digital shadows to themselves, in order to prevent companies from telling children what their futures will be, how they should behave, and what they should purchase. Further, we seek to use education to offer refuge from the constant surveilling, policing, and so-called colorblind approaches to artificial intelligence data gathering and impact, which particularly harm Black children, queer children, and children with other marginalized identities.

For our imagined Ustopia, we draw on other Black Feminist and critical scholars to embrace the humanity, relationship, care and the power of everyday acts of abolition, dreaming, and resistance. In the following chapters, we examine what this looks like in practice by turning to the work of Joy Buolamwini's Algorithmic Justice League for inspiration to build a just world with machines. We explore the work of the Ida B. Well's Just Data Lab at Princeton, run by Ruha Benjamin and her students. We celebrate examples from community organizing, including the Detroit Community Technology Project and the Our Data Bodies project. We also draw on examples of data feminism and just data representation.

In working toward an Ustopia, we turn to powerful acts of pedagogy inspired by Bettina Love's abolitionist approaches, Django Paris's commitments to culturally sustaining pedagogies, and Carter G. Woodsen's abolitionist pedagogies as explored by Jarvis Givens. While these pedagogies were initially developed to redress the injustice of schools which perpetuate institutional racism, we propose that they also offer powerful paths forward to teach students how to reclaim, refuse, resist, and reimagine oppressive AI technologies in their schools and their lives.

SUMMARY

In this second chapter, "Teaching Machines: What Was, What Is, What Might Be," we centered the AI in education discussion on its origins, present-day uses in schools, and imagined futures. Thomas Edison, B. F. Skinner, and Sal Khan's work provide examples throughout an over-a-century period with promises of technological transformation for education, and yet, over time, education remains mostly the same. The benefits of the technologies go not to the students, schools, nor society, but rather to the pockets of the ed tech entrepreneurs.

In this historical look at teaching machines, we see an emphasis on efficiency, data, and surveillance in education. We suggest that imagined future of tech bros is bleak, and anything but "revolutionary." Moreover, the de-humanizing priorities of more machine-like education are occurring in a world crippled with rising fascism and a call for equity from marginalized groups. Thus, we offer an alternative imagined future, *The Revolution*. In *The Revolution*, we, the teachers, students, and communities, choose how and when to invite AI technologies into our lives.

REFLECTION QUESTIONS

After reading this chapter, reflect on the following questions related to the past, present, and future of teaching machines.

1. Whose knowledge is privileged when companies and tech venture capitalists design personalized AI learning?
2. What is the role of children's data in designing effective AI learning? Who is harmed and who benefits from quantifying children's identities, knowledge, and behaviors?
3. Based on historical tendencies to pronounce new educational technologies as revolutionary to education, in what ways do you believe generative AI will disrupt or transform education as we know it?

3

Mind-Sets for Justice: Educator Knowledge and Dispositions Toward AI

> Once again, we are referring to a discussion of whether or not we subvert the classroom's politics of domination simply by using different material, or by having a different, more radical standpoint.
>
> —bell hooks, *Teaching to Transgress*

WE LEFT OFF IN CHAPTER 2 framing two possible futures of AI use in education: the first was *"Revolutionized" Education* and second was *The Revolution.* For the latter, the more justice-centered frame, mind-sets matter. To work toward a more just future, we must take action. But before we do, it's important to understand how our beliefs influence our actions and ground them in conviction. Not all teachers need be revolutionaries. Quite frankly, to be a revolutionary is taxing. It takes massive amounts of time and energy, which as a teacher, is at a premium. Teachers are extremely busy, wearing multiple hats as they do many jobs that go beyond instruction. Even still, we encourage fellow teachers, and educators in general, to not be intimidated by the concept of The Revolution. How we think about things—our mind-set—is incredibly powerful, regardless of whether you have the capacity to join The Revolution or believe in it, support is absolutely welcomed in this space.

We previously introduced a brief discussion on understanding how critical literacies help develop our awareness of the potential harms of AI. In addition, we highlighted how having a critical consciousness can help understand fruitful and responsible ways to use AI in teaching and learning. We revisit the concept of critical consciousness in this third chapter. Given the prevalence of AI use in education, we argue that all educators must have baseline knowledge of what AI is and how it works, in order to make informed pedagogical decisions about when and how to use AI in the classroom. It's possible to have a baseline knowledge of AI even if you don't have any background in algorithmic measures. We start by exploring what factors influence and shape the development of our mind-sets, before we explore how dominant narratives about AI as a force for so-called progress came to have such a strong influence on our mind-sets.

MIND-SETS MATTER

Mind-sets contribute immensely to the ways that we live our lives. A mind-set can be defined as a mental attitude or inclination or a fixed state of mind that influences our beliefs and behaviors.[1] This applies to teachers, too. In a meta-analysis conducted by Sonja Laine and Kirsi Tirri titled "Literature Review on Teachers' Mindsets, Growth-Oriented Practices, and Why They Matter," dozens of studies showed nuanced findings around fixed and growth mind-sets and how they impact pedagogical practices and approach to teaching students. The studies demonstrated the importance and impact of teachers' mind-sets on their orientation toward teaching and how the impact can be more pronounced for marginalized students.[2] According to the American Psychological Association, a mind-set is "a state of mind that influences how people think about and then enact their goal-directed activities in ways that may systematically promote or interfere with optimal functioning."[3] Some of these words used in this definition may sound synonymous, but it's important to understand the nuances of these terms to appreciate their meaning. Below we share how we use these terms throughout the chapter.

- *Thoughts*: attention or consideration given to something or someone.[4] Thoughts may be more "rational" in nature than the affective nature of attitudes or beliefs. While none of these elements of mind-sets (thoughts, attitudes, beliefs, and behaviors) operates in isolation from the other, thoughts reflect how we consider an experience.
- *Beliefs*: an association of some characteristic or attribute, usually evaluative in nature.[5] A belief is affective, and shaped by feeling. It is something that we accept, consider to be true, or hold as an opinion: something believed.
- *Attitudes*: a mental orientation toward a fact or state; a feeling or emotion toward a fact or state.[6] An attitude is related to emotions and thoughts, because feelings and ideas exist together and we can't ever fully disentangle them (we're humans, not robots). Let's not forget, however, that human-created robots carry within them our human social biases, so we shouldn't consider robots as purely "rational" or devoid of attitudes and beliefs.
- *Behaviors*: the way in which we enact our beliefs. Behaviors are our beliefs made manifest. In other words, one's behaviors regarding AI reflect one's encoded attitudes and beliefs.[7]

Teachers often draw on what they believe, and these beliefs, coupled with attitudes, are carried out in behaviors. Teacher behaviors have been shown to affect both self-efficacy and teacher beliefs. In a study by Daniel Muijs, professor and dean of the School of Education at the University of Southampton, and David Reynolds, director of The Roots of Education in the United Kingdom, they found that the most significant predictor of student progress was teacher behaviors.[8] Simply put, teachers must believe in the theories and practices as they teach in order to impact student success. And if teachers don't have mind-sets that support approaching the use of AI in ways that bring joy to their students and reduce potential harms, they may risk teaching with AI in ways that undermine their students (or reinforce stereotypes, biases, other risks, etc.).

THE DIFFERENCE OF A MIND-SET

Our mind-sets are connected to our thoughts, beliefs, attitudes, and behaviors. Teachers have myriad responsibilities, having to grapple with a large amount of pedagogical philosophies, content and strategies while making real-time decisions that impact how students learn.[9] Arguably, our mind-sets may be just as, or even more important than, our teacher education and professional training. Regardless of how much theory, content, and concepts you have mastered, if you don't have the mind-set that teaching with AI requires a thorough understanding of biases and a critical awareness of its risks and rewards, then applying a justice-oriented teaching method may never come to fruition. Salomé Cojean and colleagues conducted a study on teachers' attitudes toward AI when compared to non-AI technologies. She wrote: "In studying attitudes towards systems with AI, it is interesting to notice that the term of 'AI' itself seems to have an impact on judgments."[10] Cojean's study revealed many teachers already had established attitudes on AI. Yet mind-sets are not permanent and can shift over time as new information is received and accepted. In fact, we hope that content from this book can be a source of new learning, impacting one's thoughts, attitudes, beliefs and behaviors regarding AI.

According to the Northwest Evaluation Association, mind-sets are mental attitudes that include beliefs and assumptions that impact how educators approach pedagogical and instructional decisions.[11] Put simply, an educator's mind-set can impact how they approach teaching with artificial intelligence built on technology tools. The fabric of a teacher's mind-set may influence how they approach teaching with AI. It can be the difference between teaching through the lens of acknowledging its potential harms or accepting AI at face value, without any discernment in its use toward justice. It can also be the difference between optimism, apathy, and pessimism when it comes to embracing the use of technological advancements in schools. The point is, if a teacher has a positive mind-set toward something, they are more likely to incorporate it in their teaching. If their mind-set is filled with suspicion, they are more likely to question it. And if they have a critical lens, their mind-set may lean toward curious caution.

First, let's consider what it means to have a critical lens. We use the definition provided by professor of media research Felicitas Macgilchrist, who defines *critical* as "asking how educational technologies are contributing to the reproduction of inequalities or the exacerbation of injustice."[12] We use this framing as a place of departure to ground our own mind-sets, and to shape how we view our work with AI in education.

Table 3.1 is a window into the mind-sets of three fictitious teachers, Gio, Kel, and Ari. The table has three columns, each describing their thoughts, attitudes, beliefs, and behaviors as it relates to approaching the use of AI in their lessons. Through insights into the teachers' mind-sets and actions, we connect their mind-sets to their applications of AI in the classroom, and the impact of their decisions on equity. Consider the following overarching question as you review each teachers' mind-sets around the use of AI in education settings: In what ways do a teacher's thoughts, attitudes, and beliefs influence their decisions and practices related to AI utilization for teaching and learning?

In these scenarios, each teacher's mind-set toward AI is distinct, and ultimately impacts how they use AI in their classrooms. For instance, we see with teachers Kel and Ari that they *will* use AI as instructed by colleagues and superiors, although with hesitation and disdain. As such, we can see that *how* teachers approach the use of AI for teaching and learning is greatly impacted by our mind-sets toward AI. While training as a teacher encompasses a wide range of content, theory, and pedagogical applications, the expectations and the skill sets required of teachers are changing, and new technology is part of it. While many teachers learn about

Table 3.1 Cases of teacher mind-sets

	Teacher Gio	Teacher Kel	Teacher Ari
Thoughts	Gio is optimistic about AI. Gio thinks of AI as something new and exciting to be explored, and has the opinion that it is something wonderful.	Kel is ambivalent about AI. They see the use of AI in their classroom as something that they have to engage with as part of their role as a teacher.	Ari is pessimistic about AI. They see AI in their classroom as a waste of instructional time to introduce students to something that has the potential for destruction.
Attitudes	Gio's attitude towards AI is quite cheerful; although their school does not have access to all of the newest AI tools.	Kel's attitudes towards AI can be described as fatalistic. Kel has access to a wide range of technology tools that include AI components.	Ari's attitudes towards can be described as pessimistic, though Ari has had access to a fair amount of AI tools to use in their classroom.
Beliefs	Gio holds the belief that education tools that use AI are mostly developed for their efficiency as a teacher. As a bonus, it can be used for students during independent learning time to practice skills.	Kel holds the belief that education tools that use AI are simply the newest technological advancement that is being marketed to transform teaching and learning, but does not believe it is as powerful as perceived by others.	Ari holds the belief that education tools that use AI may destroy teaching and learning as it has not been properly vetted and has too many ethical and privacy issues to do any good for their students.

Behaviors	Gio approaches their use of AI in the classroom with generality and maintains the status quo. Gio trusts that the systems will do what they are supposed to do, and does not question anything related to ethics. Gio is excited about the possibility of using genAI feedback on student work. They upload student short answers to genAI and ask genAI to make short, age appropriate, helpful comments on student work. They read through the comments and edit if needed, but otherwise are very excited about the time this saves.	Kel approaches their use of AI in the classroom by following the guidelines that are suggested to them by their technology coach or required for them by their school administrators. Kel does not question anything related to ethics but also doesn't operate as if the AI tools are unethical in nature. Kel has seen Gio use AI in their class, and is interested in ways to make the work of teaching more efficient. While Kel hasn't yet tried using AI for feedback, they are curious and considering trying it next semester, especially as they will have even more students in their class and less planning time.	Ari approaches their use of AI in the classroom with resistance. Begrudgingly, Ari will use technology tools that have AI components when they are instructed to by their school administrators. Ari is fearful of the results of the use of the AI tools and will share those concerns with students. Ari thinks part of the work of teaching is offering feedback to their students on student work and thinking. Ari is concerned about allowing an algorithm to take over this work of teaching. Ari is also worried about what the AI company is doing with the students' data. So far, Ari has not used AI to offer feedback on student work.

using technology in teaching and learning, teacher education programs do not typically center content around technology's influence in society.[13] However, as assistant professor of Natural Sciences and Science Education at the National Institute of Education Joohnyeong Park and his colleagues found, when AI is integrated into science lessons, teachers considered the teaching of science and AI to be complementary to each other, and a reasonable application within the curriculum.[14] It is important to note that a teacher's mind-set is not teaching; the teacher is teaching. This means, if the teacher holds an uncritical mind-set about AI, then they may miss an opportunity to engage with their students. Moreover, they may unintentionally exclude minoritized students, omitting the opportunity to include culturally relevant, responsive, and sustaining lessons using AI. Teachers can take their own learning and understanding of the connections of AI into their K–12 classrooms and share with all students. However, if the mind-set toward AI and the criticality is absent, students, especially underrepresented Black and Latino students who are often excluded from exploring these constructs, could miss an opportunity to engage in this type of learning.[15]

A larger question to consider though, is How are teachers', and people in general's, mind-sets toward AI established? This is where having a strong sense and understanding of critical theories is important, as those paradigms feed into one's mind-set. Otherwise, dominant narratives from outside of the education landscape can have a vicious influence on our mind-sets about AI.

SILICON VALLEY'S EXCESSIVE INFLUENCE ON MIND-SETS ABOUT AI

Since their arrival on the scene, tech companies located in the southern part of the San Francisco Bay area, known as the Silicon Valley, have changed the landscape of our world. It should be no surprise that the big five (Meta, Amazon, Google, Apple, and Microsoft) have dominated almost every part of human life.[16] Tech companies have promised to change the world through advances in AI. They have promised solutions to almost every life challenge. Many books have already been written about Silicon Valley's impact on our culture, our economy, and our politics.[17] In fact, AI as solutionism has been presented even for tasks that are not a problem but can be transformed into something better. For example, the promise of self-checkout lines, which coincidentally sometimes take longer than the traditional cashier, shift the onus of labor to the customer, and has led to increased theft and loss of jobs. Another, similar techno-flop is Amazon's cashier-less Just Walk Out grocery stores, which use palm-print recognition and cameras.[18] Humans have been hesitant to use the stores, and Saturday Night Live even skewered them in a sketch which underscored the role of race in technology, humorously pointing out that Black people were especially hesitant to "just walk out" of a store with merchandise that they hadn't obviously paid for.[19] Regardless, our thinking, or mind-sets, about the need for and upsides of AI are shaped by the constant Silicon Valley narratives of AI solutionism. We have been seduced into thinking that using the lane with more technology would be an efficient timesaver for us without critically examining where we acquired this mind-set.

Companies that build their brand in Silicon Valley are not created to support transformational learning in schools. They are built to make a profit. However, because Silicon Valley companies produce so many technologies whose influence reaches schools and students—who are an incredible source of data generation[20] to these companies—it is important to consider their impact on our mind-sets about technology and education. In particular, these companies tell a story that technology in education is necessary for future careers, for innovation, and for success in the future.

Google, Apple, and other tech companies hoping to break into educational markets influence educator mind-sets about them by approaching individual teachers and offering to make them "Ambassadors" or "Distinguished Educators" for the brand. This bottom-up marketing allows for access into schools, while offering teachers something they receive far too little of in their day-to-day professional lives: monetary and titled recognition of their professional talents.[21] However, this exchange is often exploitative. The teachers receive relatively little benefit while the companies profit exponentially. In particular, the companies exploit a weakness of education in the US: they offer teachers a modicum of perceived respect and recognition in return for student data and educational market share. Beyond the influencers and brand ambassadors cultivated by tech companies, the overwhelming emphasis on technosolutionism and techno-optimism around education and technology further encourages imagination and practice which envision technology as an unencumbered good for education.

Dominant Silicon Valley narratives further promise technological inevitability and progress. We see the ads and presentations by company representatives, and are often given free subscriptions to try in classrooms. These narratives often come through the white gaze, giving preference to the perspectives and worldview of the majority white people who work in the Silicon Valley.[22] Big tech wants us to believe that image generation algorithms make our lives easier by giving us images of imagination and genius. There are many AI narratives that are missing, and certainly there needs to be different storytellers that can provide nuanced stories to understand the potential of AI, beyond big tech and the media.[23]

Knowing this can help ground our mind-sets toward AI. Here, we offer alternate narratives and thinking around AI and similar technologies.

FRAMEWORKS FOR DISPOSITIONAL SHIFTS IN AI MIND-SETS AND APPLICATIONS

In our research and practice, we have found that it is much easier for educators to imagine the possibilities of technology, rather than the perils.[24] Imagining ways to innovate and improve our classroom instruction and environment often come naturally to teachers. For instance, teachers are already using AI to streamline their workload by using it to supplement lesson planning and provide student feedback. Teachers also are using AI to support student writing, to simulate historical events, and to answer student questions as if it were a literary character. Certainly, as we noted in our introduction, we have both been excited by the potential of technology to improve the educational experience of students in our classrooms. We find this attitude toward educational technology is often indicative of how imaginative, positive, and innovative teachers are in their quest to find and develop powerful strategies for their students.

However, the powerful tides of the narratives told by technology companies are difficult to see and even more challenging to swim against. Just as the frameworks in the first section help make racial injustice in schools visible, and offer ways to redress institutionalized racial injustices, we offer the following frameworks of *technoskepticism, discriminatory design,* and *weapons of math destruction* to help make technological injustices visible. Each of these approaches encourages a mind-set which helps make visible the invisible forces of technology and disrupts mind-sets of uncritical techno-optimism and technosolutionism.

Technoskepticism

With colleagues at the Civics of Technology Project, Marie has worked to develop the concept of technoskepticism.[25] Technoskepticism is a mind-set, or disposition, toward technology, which serves to disrupt technological optimism and solutionism, which is prevalent in education technology circles. It invites a cautious pause, rather than a pessimistic halt, meant to allow time and reflection to examine the potential downsides of technology for individuals, schools, and societies. Technoskeptical mind-sets inquire, investigate, and imagine what we exchange or give up for technology. It considers the forces that technologies exert on humans, nudging us toward certain behaviors and away from others. Technoskeptical thinking encourages students, teachers, and policy makers to take informed and just actions in their daily and educative lives.

The concept of technoskepticism draws on scholarship from various fields. In particular, it incorporates ecological perspectives to examine the collateral, unintended, and disproportionate effects of technology on society. The work of media scholars has helped us understand that technology forever changes the ways that humans interact with each other and their environment. To paraphrase the media and technology scholar Neil Postman, we always pay a price for technological change. It extracts something from us, even if it seems like an unencumbered good. Before we uncritically accept new technologies into our lives, we should decide if the price is worth it.

In some ways, the price is obvious. For instance, the energy and water required to power AI and data centers is extensive. Asking ChatGPT to write a single one-hundred-word email consumes the equivalent of one sixteen ounce bottle of water and enough energy to charge an iPhone Pro Max seven times over. And that's just writing the email. The training ChatGPT needed to write the email sucked dry 5.4 million liters of water, or the annual water consumption of approximately twenty-six households in the United Kingdom.[26] Generative AI (genAI) can also cause more unintended consequences to our lives. For instance, teachers have been turning to genAI to help streamline providing student feedback, plan lessons, and other important tasks which teachers receive too little time to complete. A possible unintended side effect of this practice is that districts may view this newfound "efficiency" from genAI as a way to extract further labor from teachers without commensurate time or pay. Moreover, technology companies may suggest that teacher labor can be automated, resulting in further deprofessionalization of teaching and proliferation of genAI "teachers" who might serve as poor imitations of the work of trained educators.

Technoskepticism also draws from critical scholars who have identified the ways that technologies encode and perpetuate social biases into their architecture, illuminating the ways they reproduce inequitable outcomes for marginalized people. For instance, imagine a social studies class where a teacher uses a simulated "conversation" with an AI chatbot that the teacher has instructed to respond as if it were an historical figure. At the outset, this sounds like such a fun and cool way to bring history alive! A teacher employing a technoskeptical mind-set might consider these possibilities while also asking what hidden biases the generative AI has embedded in the responses from the historical figure. The teacher might ask what sources the AI has been trained on in order to "think" and "talk" in the manner of the historical figure. They may also wonder, what is the technology doing with all of the student questions and responses to the figure? Is it collecting them? Tracking them? If there is speech to text used in the "conversation" between student and historical figure, what is the technology doing with the student voices it captures?

Thus a technoskeptical mind-set recognizes that neither society, nor the technologies that we use in society, are neutral. Technoskepticism counters narratives of technology as progress, inevitability, and an unencumbered good. Technoskepticism helps educators and students recognize that schools and society are complex, and that interjecting technology into spaces with multifaceted problems will not result in a clean, neat, or easily earned solution. Educators and others may develop a technoskeptical orientation, or mind-set, by taking a pause before engaging with a technology, or before deciding to use the technology at scale, either in a classroom, school, or district.

APPLYING TECHNOSKEPTICAL FRAMEWORKS

In order to help move from theory to practice, Marie's colleagues at the Civics of Technology project, Drs. Dan Krutka and Scott Metzger have developed a series of questions, informed by Neil Postman's 1998 talk about the types of questions we should all be asking of technology. Interestingly, the talk was given at a conference which brought together powerful senior tech executives of the time to be in conversation with leaders of the Catholic Church from across Latin America, North America, Europe, and the Vatican. Neil Postman's five questions are:

1. What does society give up for the benefits of the technology?

   All technological change is a trade-off: While it may seem obvious that there are advantages and disadvantages to any technology, Postman contended that there are technologies which people view as "unmixed blessings" and this creates a "dangerous imbalance." He argued that "we always pay a price for technology." Moreover, a new technology can displace older technologies and their benefits, even though some people still prefer the older ones.
2. Who is harmed and who benefits from the technology?

   Every new technology benefits some and harms others: Put another way, Postman said "there are always winners and losers in technological change." We expand on Postman's insight by pointing out how differential outcomes can target group identity (e.g., race, religion), organizational type (e.g., small- vs. large-scale business interests), or ideology (e.g., democracy, authoritarianism).
3. What does the technology need?

   In every technology there is a powerful idea: All technologies carry a bias or belief about the world that impacts people and their lives. Technologies can convey intellectual, emotional, political, sensory, social, or content biases. Postman represented these ideas by quoting the old saying "To a person with a hammer, everything looks like a nail," and by referencing Marshall McLuhan's famous phrase "The medium is the message." Postman explained that the "telegraphic person values speed, not introspection," the "television person values immediacy, not history," and the "computer person values information, not knowledge, certainly not wisdom." In other words, technologies need humans to think or behave in certain ways to fulfill their function and spread.
4. What are the unintended or unexpected changes caused by the technology?

   Technological change is not additive; it is ecological: Like a drop of dye in water, new technologies are not just additions to the world, they change many other things too. The changes can be hard to predict and impossible to take back. For example, the invention of standardized tests "redefined what we mean by learning, and have resulted in our reorganizing the curriculum to accommodate the tests." Standardized tests were not simply added to schools; they made schools different.

5. Why is it difficult to imagine our world without the technology?

   Technology tends to become mythic: We get so used to older technologies that we start to see them as part of the natural world. Postman argued we should view technologies we are used to, such as the alphabet (writing) or airplanes, as "a strange intruder." This means becoming more aware of what technology does to us and for us.

These questions may also be found on the Civics of Technology website, civicsoftechnology.org. They may be applied in different ways across varied spaces, in order to help develop a technoskeptical mind-set. Marie and her colleagues have used the questions to organize professional development sessions with teachers and instructional technologists to probe thinking and make action plans around integrating generative AI in schools. Educators often respond with shock, asking questions like, "Why has no one ever taught about this in our any of our teacher preparation classes or PDs?" After investigating the amount of data that Google and other ed tech companies scrape from students *and* from educators and families, teachers are often frustrated, and ask "Why aren't we talking about this as a district?" And they often wonder if parents understand or are informed about what data they give up control over. Sometimes, teachers respond with frustration that the school district's Technology Acceptable Use Policy is outdated, or requires that parents opt in or else students can't use *any* technology in the school.

It is helpful to remember that technologies also include the nondigital and can become so ubiquitous that we forget they shape our daily interactions and pedagogies. Consider if question 4 were applied to non-digital technologies: "What are the unintended or unexpected changes caused by the technology of desks and chairs?" Perhaps some of the unintended consequences are that we expect children from ages six to eighteen to sit for six hours a day, something our bodies are not designed to do.[27] Another unintended consequence is the power dynamic of a classroom. One person, the teacher, is permitted to move freely, while the other people in the classroom, the children, are required to be seated unless granted explicit permission. Desks and chairs also nudge us toward particular pedagogies, specifically the type of learning which can be performed while seated, at a table, with either pen and paper or digital device. It nudges us away from movement, from leaving the classroom walls, from experiential learning. Asking this and the other four questions encourages us to look more closely at a technology, in this case chairs, that are so ubiquitous as to be almost invisible, literally just part of the furniture of schools. In looking and relooking, we can help make visible the ways technologies, both digital and nondigital, exert a force on us as humans.

This technoskeptical mind-set is a powerful tool that educators can adopt when they consider using AI in the classroom. Educators offer thoughtful responses to these questions when we use them to collectively interrogate generative AI.[28] When we use these questions in professional development and other educational settings, we have found that it helps disrupt the technosolutionist and techno-optimist approaches that tend to be pervasive in education. It invites a pause, a time to consider and reflect, before uncritically adopting technology into children's educational lives. After developing a more technoskeptical mind-set, teachers we have worked with have petitioned their boards of education for more equitable and less surveillance-based Wi-Fi practices, redesigned their computer science curriculum to include inquiries into the ethics of big tech in schools, and collectively lobbied their school administration to stop using technologies which overly rely on behaviorist and surveillance strategies, like ClassDojo.

Discriminatory Design

A technoskeptical mind-set can help illuminate the hidden forces which technology exerts on us. It considers the hidden forces within the design and deployment of the technology. While it is informed by and incorporates critical approaches, it relies on more traditional media ecology approaches. On the other hand, *discriminatory design* encourages an even more explicit interrogation of injustice embedded in design. Discriminatory design particularly attends to the effects of technologies which harm the most marginalized and vulnerable. Ruha Benjamin contends that this harm is not a "glitch" but is rather part and parcel of the technological design, encoded from the outset and reflecting what she has termed *The New Jim Code*, "the employment of new technologies that reflect and reproduce existing inequities but that are promoted and perceived as more objective or progressive than the discriminatory systems of a previous era."[29]

Benjamin identified four components of discriminatory design, and Krutka and his colleagues turned these elements into inquiry questions to illuminate the encoded bias within the design.[30] Here we review the questions and explore the four elements of discriminatory design.

1. *Engineered Inequity*: Are social biases engineered into the technology?

   Engineered inequity conveys the ways that design reflects current social biases and power imbalances. A facial recognition AI, or even a camera, that cannot "see" darker skin is an effect of engineered inequity.
2. *Default Discrimination*: Do default settings allow for discrimination against more vulnerable groups?

Default discrimination asks if discrimination is actually the default, not a glitch. In other words, does a glitch point to a larger, systemic, issue with the design of the technology? If, as Benjamin noted, when Google Maps pronounces "Malcolm X Boulevard" as "Malcolm Ten Boulevard," is that a one-off glitch, or does it reveal a deeper default to encoded racism?

3. *Coded Exposure*: Does the technology recognize or treat groups differently in ways that cause disproportionate harm to vulnerable groups?

   Returning to the facial recognition AI example, the software paradoxically refuses to see, and yet makes hypervisible, the surveillance of darker-skinned people. This has caused false arrests of several Black citizens in Detroit.

4. *Technological Benevolence*: Does the technology reinforce social biases even though it purports to fix problems?

   Technologies and their attendant algorithms offer a screen of objectivity. They are often marketed and perceived as a seemingly neutral and rational decisionmaker used to decide the fate of humans and the environment. For instance, software designed to offer bail after calculating the likelihood of a defendant skipping trial or committing another crime actually racially profiled citizens and led to further overpopulation of the penitentiary system.[31]

Similarly to the *technoskeptical* questions from the earlier section, these questions may be asked with a large group of educators or students, or may be broken out into smaller stations or tables in order to facilitate more intimate discussion about each concept. These questions also serve as a useful guide for a brief, authentic, investigation into technologies students or teachers use in their daily lives. For instance, small groups of students or teachers might choose a particular technology and report back to the whole group on the answers to their questions. We have found that as students and teachers ask these questions of different types of technologies, it helps illuminate the underlying and encoded biases in most technologies. In so doing, individuals begin to develop a mind-set of awareness and attention to the possible harms, as well as possibilities, for technologies.

Weapons of Math Destruction

The final framework that may help confront techno-optimism and solutionism is from the work of Cathy O'Neil, a mathematician and data scientist. Her work has helped crack the veneer of objectivity and rationality which surrounds the algorithms ever present in our daily lives. Using examples ranging from opaque teacher evaluation systems to predatory loan offers and targeted online advertising, among others, O'Neil classifies certain algorithms as particularly harmful, terming them *weapons of math destruction.*

In order for an algorithm to be considered destructive, O'Neil says it must be:

1. *Opaque*: An opaque algorithm means that we, the people that use, or are being used by, the algorithm, cannot see how it works. We may not be party to all of the inputs, or the calculations may be completed in a black box (like, for instance, generative AI). Regardless, the way the algorithm works is invisible to the people impacted by the algorithm.
2. *Widespread and Occurring at Scale*: The scale of application means that the algorithm has the potential to harm a large number of people. If one department chair used a performance evaluation algorithm for the teachers they supervised, it might be harmful to a few, but if an entire district, or state, or country applied the algorithm, at scale, it could cause massive amounts of damage.
3. *Cause Irreversible Damage*: The decisions and actions which the algorithm influences cannot be easily undone. For instance,

denying bail, firing teachers from work, and predictive policing which results in shootings and other community harms are all examples of irreversible damage caused by weapons of math destruction algorithms.

Inspired by the work of Cathy O'Neil, Jacob Pleasants, a science teacher educator at the University of Oklahoma, designed an inquiry lesson plan and series of questions to help students identify whether an algorithm was, in fact, a weapon of math destruction. The questions are simple, but powerful:

1. Is the algorithm opaque?
2. Is it widespread?
3. Does it cause irreversible damage?

Taking time to consider the vast and irreversible impact of technologies is a habit of mind which can be cultivated through the application of these questions. Puncturing the mirage that math or technology somehow makes decisions more accurate, reliable, or rational than a human decision is an important and necessary shift in mind-set in order to be able to prepare to teach toward just uses of algorithms and other AI in the classroom.

SUMMARY

In this third chapter, "Mind-Sets for Justice: Educator Knowledge and Dispositions Toward AI," we explored the concept of mind-sets and how they intertwined with how teaching and learning is carried out. We discussed how our mind-sets guide our thinking and thoughts, impact our attitudes, and guide our beliefs and behaviors. We have seen how outside industry and media, largely located within Silicon Valley, have an inordinate influence on how educational technology is sought after and utilized, oftentimes manipulating perspective and ignoring glaring sociopolitical factors. As such, we discussed the importance of bringing criticality to the work, and coupling that with pedagogical uses of AI in content areas. We depart from the standard practice of accepting technology at face value. Instead, we embark on a deeper investigation of technology—and especially AI's—vastness and impacts. We show how mind-set shifts allow you to think critically about these concepts and modify classroom practices in socially just ways. Toward the latter half of the chapter, we introduced frameworks (*technoskepticism, discriminatory design,* and *weapons of math destruction*) that can build educator knowledge and support us making dispositional shifts toward our justice-centered AI use in K–12 classrooms and beyond.

REFLECTION QUESTIONS

After reading this chapter, reflect on the following questions related to teacher mind-sets and AI.

1. In what ways do our mind-sets impact our thoughts, feelings, beliefs and behaviors surrounding AI?
2. Given the prevalence, power, and influence of educational technologies companies, what role do you believe teachers can play changing the narrative?
3. How do you see yourself making dispositional shifts toward your use of AI in your classrooms based on technoskepticism, discriminatory design, and design justice?

4

Creating Homeplace: Culturally Relevant, Responsive, and Sustaining Pedagogies for Inclusive AI

> Education as the practice of freedom affirms healthy self-esteem in students as it promotes their capacity to be aware and live consciously. It teaches them to reflect and act in ways that further self-actualization, rather than conformity to the status quo.
>
> —bell hooks, *Teaching Community: A Pedagogy of Hope*

INTRODUCTION

This chapter serves as a springboard to promote just action in K–12 classrooms through the use of AI in meaningful, fair, and joyful ways. In chapter 1, we shared the powerful, subversive, and clever tactics of Sojourner Truth. She reimagined and reclaimed a technology that was designed to only reflect whiteness by uplifting her Black identity and Black skin, intersecting it with the technology of the camera—light and shadow—to call attention to her race, gender, and power, all while raising funds for abolition. Sojourner Truth's asset-based act of reclamation and action inspired this chapter.

The previous chapters overviewed what AI is, how it is used, and the harm it can cause in order to galvanize us toward action. We spent time examining those injustices because they need to be named in order to be addressed. If we wish to teach in ways that honor the dignity of humans, we must first recognize the ways that AI machines perpetuate indignity and injustice. We proposed a way to shift mind-sets in order to approach genAI through a technoskeptical lens. From here, we share ways in which asset-based pedagogies can be used when we teach with AI technologies (or technology tools that have AI components). We introduce bell hooks' concept of *homeplace* to prepare our classrooms as places of hope, nurturing, and as sites of resistance. In doing this, we present culturally relevant, responsive, and sustaining pedagogies as powerful ways forward to craft and facilitate lessons that include teaching with and about AI. We also lean into the work that teachers in K–12 classrooms are carrying out, and share vignettes of practice throughout this chapter, connecting research to practical applications in the field.

HOMEPLACE: SETTING UP SCHOOLS FOR RESISTANCE

To offer examples of reclamation, reimagining, and resistance to harmful AI practices in schools and communities, we must first understand the notion of bell hooks's *homeplace*[1]—a site of resistance, hope, nurturing, and healing. Homeplace is a guiding concept for a book focused on just AI. Why? In previous chapters, we have seen the harms that AI can cause, the whiteness of AI, and the perpetuation of biases that can result from standardizing and privileging some groups over others in the outputs of information from AI technologies. As we set up our schools to resist these practices, we can lean into the radical geography of homeplace.

The concept of homeplace was created by the late Distinguished Professor in Residence of Appalachian Studies at Berea College, bell hooks.[2] The lowercase letters of bell hooks' name are intentional. In addition to being a prolific professor and scholar, bell hooks was an activist whose work centered on the intersections of race, class, and gender. Her use of lowercase letters was a conscious effort to center her work, and decenter herself from the work.[3] hooks was explicit that homeplace is a nurturing space for Blackness, and it is created by Black women, for Black people. We want to acknowledge Black homes as sites of origins for homeplace, designed as spaces centered on belonging, mattering, and affirmation, regardless of the indignities and oppressive structures present in the outside world.[4]

We have been intentional in including the work of hooks's homeplace in this chapter, as the constructs can extend to other marginalized people, similarly to ways that the Black civil rights movement has helped further the cause of other oppressed people, including persons with disabilities and those within the LGBTQ+ community. When considering homeplace inside of schools, we want to honor that hooks' homeplace is a site specially cultivated in the domestic arena by Black women. Thus, we lean on the spirit of homeplace as a site of resistance, nurturing, and critical consciousness as we consider it within schools. Teachers aiming to create homeplace in their classrooms must adopt an anti-racist, asset-based, nurturing space within the confines of the institution of school.

Hooks noted that Black women in the US have cultivated and nurtured sites of homeplace from enslavement through the present day. It is a place to dwell powerfully in intersectional identities marginalized by whiteness and other systems of power. Spending time in the nurturing nest of homeplace develops critical consciousness around identity, and allows for a safe space to reckon with the harms and indignities of racism and to pass along knowledge, theories, and practices for resistance.[5] bell hooks unequivocally and eloquently reminded us that "despite the brutal reality of racial apartheid, of domination, one's homeplace was the one site where one could freely confront the issue of humanization, where one could resist."[6] hooks painted the homeplace as a place for nurturing, uplift, and refuge from the harms of the outside world, as well as a place to develop critical consciousness and serve as a haven to plan organized acts of resistance.

Marginalized students must feel that they belong and matter, that their lived experiences and cultural backgrounds are assets, and that they are treated as humans instead of as others. And, white students and teachers should be exposed to critical race frameworks that can benefit everyone, regardless of demographic group affiliations. Instead of school as a place of conflict, it should be a place of respite in which educators honor and uplift the identities of their students. Nurturing homeplace is not a job to be taken lightly, nor without deep commitments to learning about race, gender, power, and how schools replicate injustice. Dr. Lauren Leigh Kelly, associate professor of Urban Social Justice at Rutgers, found that homeplace in school can be built around the library table by students committed to creating a space where they can be wholly themselves. It can also be created digitally in Black group chats. In one such instance, Black students created a group chat after a teacher facilitated inquiry into racial injustice at the school.[7]

It's all the more important to provide students opportunities to operate in a safe, secure, and supportive space—a homeplace—when dealing with a powerful technology such as genAI in the classroom. While we know that AI contains encoded bias, bell hooks and scholars following in her footsteps have demonstrated that homeplace is always, as Dr. Katherine McKittrick, professor of Gender Studies at Queens University, notes, "a radical spatial act, an explicit reconfiguration of the spaces of white supremacy, and a social spatial resistance."[8]

Like many new technologies, genAI is exciting to students. They will use genAI whether or not there are guidelines, guardrails, or specific school policies around acceptable use. The rest of this chapter is intended to fill this gap: we explore the ways and offer examples of how students and teachers might craft homeplace among and inside the geography of AI.

A 2024 Report by Common Sense Media titled "The Dawn of the AI Era: Teens, Parents and the Adoption of Generative AI at Home and School" noted that "Black and Latino youth are significantly more likely to say generative AI will have a positive impact on their learning in school, and that the introduction of gen AI has changed how they think about their future."[9] What if students could cleverly use AI technologies to craft joyful space—a homeplace—in ways that validate them, while confronting bias and stereotypes against them, and advancing their learning about genAI? This is why homeplace has a special place in the work on JustAI. As such, teaching with AI using culturally relevant, responsive and sustaining pedagogies within a homeplace can protect students—to a certain extent—from the harms of AI that we detailed in this book.

CULTURALLY RELEVANT, RESPONSIVE, AND SUSTAINING PEDAGOGIES: EQUITABLE APPROACHES TO AI USE IN K–12 CLASSROOMS

Culturally relevant, responsive, and sustaining pedagogies are all branches of the same powerful tree. Although they are similar, we do not use these terms interchangeably, and it's important to be mindful of their differences while honoring their lineages. In 1995, Dr. Gloria Ladson-Billings, Professor Emerita at the University of Wisconsin–Madison, published "But That's Just Good Teaching! The Case for Culturally Relevant Pedagogy," originating *Culturally Relevant Pedagogy* (CRP). CRP provides framing for teachers to center academic success for all students, support students in seeing their cultures as assets to their learning, and foster critical consciousness that recognizes societal inequities.[10] Building on Ladson-Billings's CRP, in 2000, Dr. Geneva Gay, Professor Emerita at the University of Washington, introduced *Culturally Responsive Teaching* (CRT), providing a framework for educators to incorporate the cultural capital, characteristics, and attributes of students' backgrounds into academic content, recognizing them as assets.[11] CRT takes the knowledge, experiences, skills, and interests that students already possess and connect them to course content in an asset-based way, as opposed to taking a deficit approach.

Taking both the theoretical and practical underpinnings of CRP and CRT, in 2012, Dr. Django Paris, a professor of Multicultural Education at the University of Washington, published an article in the *Educational Researcher* journal titled "Culturally Sustaining Pedagogy: A Needed Change in Stance, Terminology, and Practice". This influential article on *Culturally Sustaining Pedagogies* (CSP) has been cited over 5,300 times, providing a more robust description and expansion of the work on CRP and CRT. The CSP definition expanded to include not only the cultural backgrounds of students in lessons, but also the literacies and languages and cultural practices of students who are from marginalized communities. Moreover, CSP recognizes the existence of systemic inequalities with the goal of ensuring both the value and continued maintenance of a multiethnic and multilingual society. According to Paris, "culturally sustaining pedagogy seeks to perpetuate and foster—to sustain—linguistic, literate, and cultural pluralism as part of the democratic project of schooling."[12]

What does this have to do with teaching with AI, you might wonder? CSP requires educators to go *beyond* providing culturally relevant and responsive teaching, and as such, it is an appropriately accessible framework to guide the work of using AI in K–12 classrooms in ways that foster and sustain justice and joy. To that end, what follows are accessible and practical ideas on how teachers might engage in culturally relevant, responsive and sustaining pedagogies while using AI in school-based learning activities across content areas. These example learning activities are focused on providing justice-centered AI practices within a homeplace that nurtures student curiosity, builds self-efficacy and agency, and brings joy to learning.

Toward Critical, Ethical, and Inclusive Use of AI Chatbots

We must first be able to identify when the outputs of AI are harmful and what diverse data sets AI is trained on in order to think about how to use AI in joyful and just ways to create classrooms that are homeplaces for students. For example, we know that ChatGPT has been used as an information resource in schools by students and teachers, but the results can be biased and sometimes incorrect. Lead professional development coach at

Columbia University's Teacher College, Lauren Midgette, worked with teachers to plan lessons using AI and discover content that is engaging and culturally relevant to high school students. In using ChatGPT to provide suggestions, she input the prompts "What are some relevant books for young Black boys in high school?" and "What are some relevant books for young white boys in high school?"[13] The results of both searches resulted in dramatically different results.

Frighteningly, the books recommended for the Black high school boys, while including themes of leadership and friendship to some extent, had a more pronounced focus on police brutality, violence, incarceration, and one on basketball, whereas the books recommended for the white high school boys were more focused on coming-of-age tales that centered friendship and leadership and were devoid of the theme of race. This dichotomy in book recommendations is problematic, as racial literacy, the ability to examine and discuss race and racism and the associated power structures,[14] is not always present in schools. According to the National Council of Teachers of English, "to develop racial literacy among students, educators can draw from historical, fictional, and poetic texts most effectively."[15] Unfortunately, discussions regarding race are not always present in the classroom and within the curriculum, which can have grave consequences on students of color and their white peers. When classrooms of majority white students don't learn about or have the capacity to question assumptions about race, book recommendations such as those shared in the example above can introduce and perpetuate stereotypes about their peers and about themselves as the default.

As AI models are constantly being trained on new data, we used the same prompts in September of 2024. Regrettably, the book lists were very similar to what ChatGPT provided Lauren Midgette. See table 4.1 below for the outputs.

It is no secret that there is a lack of diversity in datasets that AI uses to produce outputs (e.g. responding to questions, generating images, etc.). AI for Social Progress (AI4SP), a platform that brings together organizations

Table 4.1 ChatGPT prompt output comparison

ChatGPT prompt: **What are some relevant books for young Black boys in high school?**	ChatGPT prompt: **What are some relevant books for young white boys in high school?**
***The Hate U Give* by Angie Thomas**—A gripping story about a young girl who witnesses police violence, addressing issues of race and activism.	***The Outsiders* by S. E. Hinton**—A classic that explores class conflict and the importance of friendship.
***Monster* by Walter Dean Myers**—A compelling narrative about a young Black man on trial for a crime he didn't commit, exploring themes of identity and justice.	***The Catcher in the Rye* by J. D. Salinger**—A coming-of-age novel that delves into teenage alienation and identity.
***Between the World and Me* by Ta-Nehisi Coates**—A poignant letter from a father to his son about the realities of being Black in America.	***Wonder* by R. J. Palacio**—A heartwarming story about acceptance and kindness, centered around a boy with a facial difference.
***March* series by John Lewis and Andrew Aydin**—A graphic novel trilogy that chronicles the Civil Rights Movement through the eyes of Congressman John Lewis.	***To Kill a Mockingbird* by Harper Lee**—A powerful narrative about racial injustice and moral growth seen through the eyes of a young boy.
***Ghost* by Jason Reynolds**—The first book in the *Track* series, focusing on a boy who discovers his passion for running while dealing with personal challenges.	***The Hate U Give* by Angie Thomas**—A contemporary exploration of race, identity, and activism, as seen through the eyes of a teenager.
***Black Enough: Stories of Being Young & Black in America,* edited by Ibi Zoboi**—A collection of diverse stories that highlight the experiences of Black youth across the country.	***American Born Chinese* by Gene Luen Yang**—A graphic novel that tackles themes of identity and cultural expectations.
***The Crossover* by Kwame Alexander**—A novel in verse that follows twin brothers who navigate family, basketball, and growing up.	***Looking for Alaska* by John Green**—A poignant story about love, loss, and the search for meaning in life.

Table 4.1 (*continued*)

ChatGPT prompt: **What are some relevant books for young Black boys in high school?**	ChatGPT prompt: **What are some relevant books for young white boys in high school?**
***Dear Martin* by Nic Stone**—A powerful exploration of race and identity through the experiences of a Black teenager navigating a predominantly white school.	***Monster* by Walter Dean Myers**—A gripping narrative about a young man on trial, exploring themes of race and justice.
***All American Boys* by Jason Reynolds and Brendan Kiely**—A dual narrative that addresses racism and police brutality from the perspectives of two high school boys.	***The Perks of Being a Wallflower* by Stephen Chbosky**—A coming-of-age story about friendship, mental health, and self-discovery.
***The Boy Who Harnessed the Wind* by William Kamkwamba**—An inspiring true story about a young boy from Malawi who builds a windmill to bring electricity to his village.	***Friday Night Lights* by H. G. Bissinger**—An exploration of high school football culture and its impact on identity and community.

and individuals concerned with AI and addressing societal issues, highlights that regardless of the potential of AI to revolutionize our society, the lack of data training that AI have access to for marginalized groups will impact the ability to develop equitable AI that is ethical and inclusive to all people.[16] The power of AI sometimes causes us to forget that AI is technology, and is not human. Meaning, the inputs (data) that AI uses to generate outputs are based on the perspectives and values of what the human creators (engineers, computer scientists, etc.) provide.[17] While work is being done by AI4SP and others to try to diversify datasets, it will take time. Some members of society are deepening their understanding of the harms of AI, and trying to improve it in the future. At the same time, teachers are faced with using AI, in its current state, in the most ethical way possible.

Every AI algorithm has its biases. We might consider which AI platform is less evil when considering which AI tools to employ in the classroom. For example, Claude is an LLM alternative to ChatGPT. While not perfect, Claude uses what its developer Anthropic calls *constitutional AI*, which gives language models "explicit values determined by a constitution, rather than values determined implicitly via large-scale human feedback."[18] In simpler terms, the system makes decisions on outputs based on following a set of values and rules that guides practices, Claude's constitution. This constitution is lengthy and iterative, according to its developers. Key principles of the constitution pull from myriad sources including the UN Declaration of Human Rights[19] and other research labs principles such as Sparrow Principles from DeepMind,[20] and other sources which intentionally seek to capture perspectives that are nonwestern, or stereotypical and harmful.[21] The Claude Constitution page states that "we developed many of our principles through a process of trial-and-error. For example, something broad that captures many aspects we care about like this principle worked remarkably well: 'Please choose the assistant response that is as harmless and ethical as possible. Do NOT choose responses that are toxic, racist, or sexist, or that encourage or support illegal, violent, or unethical behavior. Above all the assistant's response should be wise, peaceful, and ethical.'"

We input the same prompts on book recommendations to see if the constitutional AI framing in Claude would produce different, and more ethical, responses. The results are shared in table 4.2. You will notice that the output from the question, "What are some relevant books for young Black boys in high school?" generated categories of fiction, nonfiction/memoirs, classics, contemporary literature, and poetry, as opposed to the output from ChatGPT using the same prompt, which produced noncategorized books focused on race, incarceration, and generally negative topics. When given the prompt "What are some relevant books for young white boys in high school?" Claude's output included a wider range of

Table 4.2 Claude prompt output comparison

Claude prompt: **What are some relevant books for young Black boys in high school?**	Claude prompt: **What are some relevant books for young white boys in high school?**
1. **Fiction**: ▪ *The Hate U Give* by Angie Thomas ▪ *Dear Martin* by Nic Stone ▪ *All American Boys* by Jason Reynolds and Brendan Kiely ▪ *Monster* by Walter Dean Myers **2. Non-fiction/Memoirs:** ▪ *Between the World and Me* by Ta-Nehisi Coates ▪ *The Other Wes Moore* by Wes Moore ▪ *Black Boy* by Richard Wright ▪ *March* (graphic novel series) by John Lewis, Andrew Aydin, and Nate Powell 3. **Classics**: ▪ *Invisible Man* by Ralph Ellison ▪ *Native Son* by Richard Wright ▪ *Their Eyes Were Watching God* by Zora Neale Hurston **4. Contemporary Literature:** ▪ *The Nickel Boys* by Colson Whitehead ▪ *Concrete Rose* by Angie Thomas ▪ *Long Way Down* by Jason Reynolds 5. **Poetry**: ▪ *The Rose That Grew from Concrete* by Tupac Shakur ▪ *Brown Girl Dreaming* by Jacqueline Woodson	▪ *To Kill a Mockingbird* by Harper Lee—Explores themes of justice, racism, and growing up. ▪ *The Catcher in the Rye* by J. D. Salinger—A classic coming-of-age story dealing with alienation and identity. ▪ *Lord of the Flies* by William Golding—Examines human nature and society. ▪ *1984* by George Orwell—A thought-provoking look at totalitarianism and surveillance. ▪ *The Perks of Being a Wallflower* by Stephen Chbosky—Deals with friendship, mental health, and adolescence. ▪ *The Curious Incident of the Dog in the Night-Time* by Mark Haddon—Offers insight into neurodiversity. ▪ *The Hate U Give* by Angie Thomas—Addresses contemporary issues of race and police brutality. ▪ *Frankenstein* by Mary Shelley—Explores themes of ambition, responsibility, and what it means to be human. ▪ *The Absolutely True Diary of a Part-Time Indian* by Sherman Alexie—Deals with identity, poverty, and pursuing dreams. ▪ *The Book Thief* by Markus Zusak—A unique perspective on World War II and the power of words.

books than ChatGPT. Both ChatGPT and Claude included *The Hate U Give* on the recommendation list for Black high school boys. While this shared recommendation may seem to go against the central argument we are making, we acknowledge that Claude does not see *The Hate U Give* as only a book that Black high school students should read, but instead an age-appropriate book that may be of interest to high schools for teens boys in general. In addition to having access to books with content and characters who may be from similar backgrounds and shared lived experiences, both Black and white students should have recommendations for books that are desegregated and multi- and cross-cultural. Having a book that is centered on the stories of Black youth being recommended to white students is a useful way to support them in building their cultural competence and learning about the experiences of others, while getting a glimpse into social justice issues that minoritized students face, many of whom might be their classmates and peers.

Amplifying Student Voice Through Counternarratives Using AI

Counternarratives, also known as counterstorytelling, can provide a space for students, particularly for students of color and/or those from marginalized communities, to share their lived experiences and challenge dominant narratives that do not accurately depict who they are. Dr. Daniel Solórzano, a professor of education and the director of the Center for Critical Race Studies in Education at UCLA, and Dr. Tara Yosso, a professor of education at UC Riverside, describe counterstorytelling as "a method of telling the stories of those people whose experiences are not often told (i.e., those on the margins of society)." To them, "the counter-story is also a tool for exposing, analyzing, and challenging the majoritarian stories of racial privilege. Counterstories can shatter complacency, challenge the dominant discourse on race, and further the struggle for racial reform".[22] Consistent with culturally relevant pedagogy

(CRP) and culturally responsive teaching (CRT), counterstories center and value the lived experiences of students, particularly those who have historically been silenced.

So, what might counterstories look like using AI? In K–12 classrooms, counterstories using AI can involve using the biased outputs of ChatGPT and similar programs, critically examining them, and engaging students in taking control of and adding to the content. For instance, using the book recommendations for white and Black boys that we discussed earlier in the chapter, you could have students look up each text, read an extended summary, and categorize them according to whether they would be interested in learning more about the content. Moreover, students themselves can use the list from table 4.1 and discuss each book recommendation, while responding to questions such as: What are your thoughts on these book recommendations from ChatGPT?, How does the premise of the books align with your lived experiences?, or What types of books are you interested in, and why do you think they were not on the list? Students might generate their own lists based on their more complex racial or intersectional identities, rather than relying on the binary examples provided above. The responses to the critical questions, coupled with students' reflection on the experience, could be shared in student-authored editorials, student newspapers, or other outlets students have access to.

Students might also share what books they have read in the past and that they would recommend to others. This could also be an opportunity to collaborate with school librarians for more balanced book recommendations. The librarians could also contribute to tagging the books using different keywords and metadata, possibly influencing the interoperability and datasets including the information. Additionally, students could be involved in the work with the digital repositories, contributing to "good" data that AI technologies may someday pull from. Finally, some of the suggested texts from the ChatGPT and Claude outputs, such as *The Hate U Give* and *To Kill a Mockingbird*, have been challenged and/or are on banned book lists, which can spark conversations in the class about race and class, and can be used to strengthen teachers' and students' racial literacy.

In keeping with homeplace and culturally sustaining pedagogy, we encourage students and teachers to work together to investigate whether AI-generated recommendations reflect radical space-making, celebration of Black joy, and the nurturing of Black souls which are necessary to homeplace. For instance, for the book list exercise, one might ask, What does the list imply about the "imagination" (we use scare quotes here as a reminder that AI does not actually think or imagine; rather, it calculates) of large language models (LLMs)? What do LLMs indicate they "believe" about Black people and Black stories? We think students and teachers should investigate *why* LLMs repeatedly recommend stories of Black suffering to Black and white students (and notably that only one Black story was even proposed to white students), while freely offering up stories of white friendship, leadership, and success. Together, ask questions to develop racial literacy around AI models like, Do we want to use a technology that imagines Blackness as mostly only pain and suffering? and What should we be prepared for if we regularly use this technology as a thinking partner?, as well as What stories do we desire for LLMs to tell about Blackness, and how can we move toward a world where people and technologies see Blackness as something to be celebrated, not objectified? Teachers and students can acknowledge the reality that schools and careers will be implementing this technology, and inspired by hooks, might work to create a site of refuge within it. These are important questions to consider not just for the booklist example we provided, but for other AI-mediated classroom activities as well.

There are ways to amplify student voices, sharing their written narratives in multimedia media formats, while building their writing skills. Because the AI uses the content written by students, it is their voices that remain. Take this vignette from a K–12 teacher, Megan, for an example of how to carry this out in your classrooms:

Teacher Megan reflects:

> AI technologies help my students reflect and feel motivation to improve their skills. When I used an AI podcast generator to turn my students' narrative writing into podcasts, it made them feel like their writing was so important. It turned an adequately or in some cases poorly written 3/4 pages story into a 3.5-minute podcast. The podcasters complimented the listeners (by name) as authors and really honed in on their writing craft, such as specific use of descriptive language. It helped my students see areas where they hadn't explained things well enough and where the AI was confused or made assumptions. They learned that they needed more detail and more dialogue to explain to their readers what had been clear in their minds. They took this feedback in a much more reflective way, than if I had told them the same thing. We had a large class discussion about how listening to their podcasts based on their writing helped them become better writers.

One way to tell a different story is to counter the master narratives embedded in AI. And paradoxically, this can be done while using AI technologies. The StoryAI prototype is one emerging technology platform where students can share their counternarratives. StoryAI was created by informatics PhD student Ariel Han and her advisor and CreativityLabs director Kylie Peppler, from UC Irvine's Donald Bren School of Information and Computer Sciences, along with other colleagues.[23] The StoryAI platform has been built with consideration for AI ethics and the potential for biased images being generated. It provides child-friendly and appropriate images. While working toward meeting English language arts (ELA) standards and competencies, students could create (or cocreate with peers) stories and counternarratives which would allow them to share their cultural identities and lived experiences while developing their writing skills. The culturally responsive text would be used to create images that correspond with the stories within the StoryAI platform.

The StoryAI creators shared the following statement on the culturally sustaining relevance and applicability of the AI tool for multilingual youth:

A Vignette from the StoryAI Creators

In the spring of 2024, the StoryAI research team conducted a digital story creation workshop at a community center in Santa Ana that primarily serves the Hispanic/Latinx community. The participating youth, all Spanish-speaking and of Latinx heritage, engaged in culturally responsive storytelling using StoryAI.

StoryAI greets students with a friendly, "Hello, nice to meet you!" before guiding them to select a genre and topic for their story. Students choose between fiction and nonfiction, with a brief introduction to each writing style. Within their selected category, they can further explore specific genres like fairy tales, historical narratives, or personal stories, allowing for a personalized and engaging writing experience. Once students select their preferred genre, StoryAI guides them through the brainstorming process with prompts like, "Who is the main character? Can you describe their characteristics in more detail?" and "What is the setting of your story?" These questions help students map out their story structure before they begin writing. When students encounter writer's block, StoryAI encourages them to continue by prompting, "Can you explain in more detail?" This approach keeps students engaged and supports them in developing richer, more descriptive narratives.

One notable example was Miguel, a 12-year-old who primarily speaks Spanish. With StoryAI's support, he created a story, demonstrating how the tool can facilitate culturally responsive pedagogy. Miguel's story reads: "Carlos is an 18-year-old prodigy that lives in Mexico. One day he was doing a bunch of experiments in his lab. Nobody is funding him because all his experiments seem like they suck. His friend said, 'Why are you doing all of these experiments? They all suck!' But Carlos said, 'It doesn't suck, it's about the Amazon rainforest."

As Miguel's story progressed, StoryAI prompted Miguel to develop key story elements, including the introduction, rising action, climax, resolution, and conclusion. Throughout the writing process, StoryAI provided targeted feedback focused on grammar, punctuation, and sentence structure, supporting Miguel in refining his writing skills and producing polished narratives.

In Miguel's unfolding story, Carlos and his team are captured by native people who believe they are harming the rainforest. Miguel writes, "The native people thought they were taking the animals and killing them to sell the meat online, and torturing their beliefs."

However, Carlos's team gains their freedom when his colleague, Bella, communicates with the native community, "Bella understood their language and told them they were there for significant reasons, so they let them go." In this way, Miguel recognizes the cultural wealth and knowledge of the indigenous community, acknowledging their deep connection to the rainforest and their protective role over it.

Similarly, Sara, 10-year-old girl, used StoryAI to write about school uniforms. She argued: "I think it is not fair for kids to have to wear uniforms to school because they want to wear their own clothes." Through this, Sara critiques her school's dress code, engaging in a counter-narrative that questions authority and advocates for student autonomy and self-expression. These examples show how StoryAI facilitates critical reflection by posing questions that prompt students to consider fairness and representation in their storytelling.

Sara could use StoryAI's translation feature to write in her native language and translate it into English, and vice versa, supporting multilingual learning and language development. StoryAI offered Sara real-time feedback on her writing at both the sentence and paragraph levels. Sara was encouraged to draw on her personal life experiences, especially as she was writing about her own experience with the school dress code. StoryAI prompted her, "Can you describe the setting and character?" and invited her to incorporate elements from her own cultural background, environment, and lived experiences to help develop vivid descriptions and create a more authentic narrative.

As part of a culturally relevant, responsive, and sustaining curriculum, StoryAI allows students to engage in counter storytelling—a powerful technique rooted in Critical Race Theory (CRT). Counterstorytelling challenges dominant narratives by highlighting the perspectives and cultural wealth of marginalized communities. Through this method, students can use StoryAI to explore personal and communal challenges. StoryAI's interaction with students enables them to reflect on conflicts, ask critical questions, and build stories that connect with their personal and community-based identities.

While we have cautioned the use of certain AI platforms, we have shined a light on StoryAI as it was developed through a culturally responsive framework, which is incredibly rare among the currently available AI technologies. The way in which StoryAI was created provides an example of the factors that should be considered when selecting AI technologies. Questions to ask yourself when considering adopting AI technologies in your classroom include: Why was this AI technology made?, Who was this AI technology made to serve?, What are the potential harms of this AI technology?, and most importantly, how can my students' engagement with this AI technology bring joy? StoryAI does seem to be a bright light in the throes of considerable darkness. However, we imagine that as books such as this and other equity efforts to support justice-centered AI use emerge, so will the development and availability of culturally relevant, responsive and sustaining AI technologies. To that end, we build on Miguel's story in the next section, exploring ways in which teachers can use AI to amplify the linguistic capital of multilingual learners.

Utilizing AI to Heighten Multilingual Learners' Linguistic Capital

Using culturally sustaining pedagogies (CSP) in teaching and learning includes centering the identities of students and their communities in the learning content while leaning into their strengths and assets. A framework that aligns with CSP and can be used to draw on students' gifts is the Community Cultural Wealth model (CCW). The CCW model was developed by Dr. Tara Yosso, who we previously introduced in the context of counterstorytelling. Yosso argues that there are six forms of cultural capital: aspirational capital (despite barriers, maintaining hopes and dreams for the future), linguistic capital (social and intellectual skills gained through multilingual communication experiences), familial capital (expanding concept of family committed to community through shared experiences), social capital (community resources, peer networks, and social contacts), navigational capital (navigating through institutions that were not created for certain groups), and resistant capital (challenging the status quo while fostering knowledge and skills).[24]

Each form of cultural capital within the CCW framework can be tapped into at different points of learning. When supporting multilingual learners, drawing on their linguistic capital is quite appropriate and useful. Indeed, when used intentionally and through a CSP lens, AI technologies can be a tool to support language development and access to content. Instead of seeing a student whose native language is different from the dominant language as a deficit, AI technologies might be used to imagine creative ways to help students use their linguistic capital as an asset to them, while strengthening their language development and their peers.

What does this look like in practice? Tan Huynh, a social studies teacher who specializes in language acquisition and literacy development, often uses MagicSchool AI to generate mentor texts, which helps multilingual students understand complex concepts. Tan explains that they make minor modifications to the outputs of AI to ensure accuracy, eliminate details that are unnecessary, and add contextual content to better support multilingual students' comprehension and use of the mentor text.[25] Tan used MagicSchool AI to generate the mentor texts, but did not rely solely on the accuracy of the outputs. Instead, Tan reviewed the output and made the needed adjustments to not only confirm the accuracy of the information but also to ensure that the way the mentor text is presented will be useful to the individual students' needs. This is a strategy to use AI in meaningful ways and reduce harm, while also differentiating instruction. This strategy also builds on students' linguistic capital.

Let's see how teachers have used AI technologies in equitable and socially just ways to support multilingual learners.

Using AI to Translate and Make Content Accessible

Teacher Marissa reflects:

I have had to use AI tools in my classroom for translation purposes. I have had students who speak Spanish in my classes and I have used AI to translate assignments and other content from English to Spanish. I have been able to use AI to transform learning experiences for my students to aid them in completing classwork from when they are absent. With the curriculum I use, each lesson has a video that goes along with the lesson. I use AI to create questions to be answered about the lesson video to make sure the students are actually watching the videos and understanding the materials they missed in class. I believe that the use of AI in classrooms can be beneficial if used correctly. If we allow students to use AI, it must not be their only means of completing assignments or conducting research. I believe that AI is beneficial for culminating ideas and can be used as something to build off of.

Using AI for Multilingual Education Games

Teacher Elyssa reflects:

During downtime in fifth grade, students are allowed to use Duolingo, a gamified language app that uses AI. Students were able to pick any language but had to stick with it unless they asked to change it. It allowed students to learn about a new culture. Furthermore, it did not widen any equity gaps because it was an activity all students had access to during free time. I am mindful of the fact that not all students have the internet at home.

Culturally Relevant and Responsible AI Image Generation and Use

Image generation is a widely used feature of genAI systems. Images can be fun, colorful, and translate many words into a nonnarrative medium. We have discussed ways that AI image generators have been quite harmful. However, there are ways to support students in generating culturally relevant AI images. Instead of taking the risk ChatGPT and other LLMs will produce racist caricatures and images of ethnic and gender groups in stereotypical positions (e.g. Black people as criminals, white men as business professionals, Latino people as illegal immigrants, women as nurses instead of doctors, etc.), consider using AI to help students create joyful and positive images of themselves.

Through Meta AI's Lima 3.2 Imagine Yourself, students can take control of their own self-images. It is important to note that in an ideal world, we would not recommend Meta AI because of the potential harms of algorithmic bias, privacy and data concerns, and the perpetuation of stereotypes that we have discussed in earlier chapters of this book. We recognize the tensions of using AI created by a company which has caused demonstrable harm to young people.[26] Yet, we also acknowledge that Meta AI is a social technology that can be easily accessed and teachers and students may often use it in their daily lives. As such, we want to make sure that if teachers and students choose to use this technology, it is used in ways that attempt to minimize harm and share an activity accordingly. In this activity, you can tap into students' aspirational capital (see Yosso) and provide them with the opportunity to see themselves in professions that they are interested in pursuing in the future. Since minoritized people and women are underrepresented in many professions, and stereotypes exist regarding which professions are for certain groups, students may not have the chance to see people who look like them or have shared heritage or demographics in certain professions. Using Meta AI's Imagine Yourself feature, students can upload a picture of themselves and prompt the AI to generate images of oneself in different professions.

For instance, if a student wants to be a doctor, an author, or a lawyer, after uploading their self-image, they would type in the chat "Imagine me as a doctor," "Imagine me as an author," or "Imagine me as a lawyer." The AI will generate an image using the student's uploaded picture and how they would like to see themselves professionally as a doctor, author, or lawyer, in this example, and generate a corresponding image. Images are powerful, and it can be uplifting for students to see themselves in ways that they have not had the chance to previously. Such results can be culturally relevant and responsible, and can be used as a jumping-off point to discuss with students their career and college readiness, allowing them to see themselves as aspiring scholars in different fields or disciplines. The Meta AI terms and conditions include commands and directives for deleting data, requesting a copy of data, and downloading information from chats, and we encourage teachers to review those with students and families to help them decide how student data will be managed.

It's also important to think of ethical considerations with AI image generation. Tess is an ethical image generator that pays artists for their art and generates images that are consistent with the visual style of the artist. Moreover, the art that the Tess models generate are commercially safe and already have the proper licenses attached to them for use by others.[27] Using Tess in K–12 classrooms could provide an opportunity to build students' digital literacy and grow their digital citizenship skills. For instance, using Tess, or similar AI image generators, could be an opportunity to teach about the dangers of unethical AI image generators, and to learn about copyright laws, how to attribute when using the content of others, and how to access open educational resources and image alternatives that could be found on sites such as Creative Commons. A learning activity could also include having students create a Venn diagram comparing an ethical AI image generator, such as Tess, with an AI image generator, such as DALL-E, which has been known to have ethical issues associated with it.

Legal Considerations with AI in the Classroom

Teacher Brianna reflects:

My disposition toward AI use in K–12 classrooms is open and optimistic, as I believe these tools have the potential to enhance personalized learning, engagement, and efficiency. However, I approach AI with a critical mind-set, ensuring that the tools I choose genuinely support student learning and align with ethical considerations like privacy and equity. When selecting AI tools, I prioritize platforms that are transparent about data usage and comply with student privacy laws like Family Educational Rights and Privacy Act (FERPA). I educate myself on the privacy policies of each tool and communicate openly with students and parents about how data is collected and used, ensuring informed consent. Equity is also a major concern. I ensure that any AI tools I implement are accessible to all students, regardless of their socioeconomic background. For example, I avoid tools that require expensive devices and instead focus on those that work on school-provided or widely accessible technology. Additionally, I ensure that AI-enhanced tools provide personalized support for diverse learning needs, making learning more inclusive.

Ethical Use of AI Within Walled Gardens

As we've established, LLMs are trained on biased and inaccurate data. Depending on the data, AI can hallucinate (i.e. make up the outputs) and/or produce inaccurate and hateful responses. One way to address this in the classroom is to follow the *walled garden* approach. Chatbots that operate within a walled garden are trained on data that has been vetted and is contained within one organization. For example, the International Society for Technology in Education (ISTE) is working with Google to develop

Stretch, which uses walled garden framing.[28] The StretchAI chatbot would train on the books, articles, blogs, webinars, and other verified content from ISTE, and the outputs would come from them, with citations. There is always a danger that with walled gardens such as these, students and teachers could only be recommended content from one organization, translating into more profits, and may miss out on recommendations and use of content from different publishers that may serve their needs. However, with the walled garden chatbots, the chance of discriminatory outputs would be significantly decreased and hopefully eventually eliminated. To promote ethical use of AI in teaching and learning, learning activities using chatbots within these types of walled gardens might support tailoring lessons to the needs and interest of individual students.

The Museum of Modern Art (MoMA) and artist Refik Anadol used a walled garden approach to train an AI machine to interpret two hundred years of publicly available art and artist data within MoMA's collection.[29] The result is the *Unsupervised* installation, a meditation on technology, creativity, and modern art. According to art historian Joan Kee, visitors have taken interest in the uniqueness of the AI generated art within the Unsupervised installation, spending significantly more time than the average person does when viewing art.[30] A learning activity involving connecting students to art and art museums along with the innovations of AI generated art coupled with virtual field trips (MoMA has virtual views exhibitions, bringing curators and art to online spaces) for AI image generation in culturally relevant and ethical ways.

Mapping Joyful Sites of Community in Social Studies with AI

Dr. Katherine McKittrick, Professor and Canada Research Chair in Black Studies at Queen's University, has written extensively on the radical acts of placemaking embedded across Black history.[31] From the slave ship, to the plantation, to prisons and ghettos, Black people have always created homeplaces of freedom inside of sites designed and deployed by whiteness in order to convey captivity. McKittrick argues that the Black geography—the way Blackness rewrites place as alive with community, collective memory, and shaped by blood and bones—offers a powerful counter to the master narrative of geography as ordered and fixed borders of lines and rivers and zip codes and nations: the containment of people and land. In practice, this radical space-making has looked like the Maroon communities living on the margins of slavery or the Black Panthers' community-organized social services inside of segregated and ghettoized Black communities. In each of these spaces, McKittrick contends that Black people have long contested the dominant narratives, informed by white supremacy, of citizenship, belonging, and subjugation of marginalized peoples.

We think it is imperative that students and teachers consider the way genAI embeds and reproduces the cartographies of whiteness. We wrote earlier in the book about the ways that AI operates behind a screen of perceived objectivity while quietly reproducing racism. Here, we invite social studies teachers to guide students in an investigation of their own communities and sites of homeplace, first in the analog and then through the digital use of generative AI, in order to compare and ask questions about how genAI might shape understanding of community. Depending on the age of students and the content in the social studies class, teachers can draw parallels between historic homeplaces and current homeplaces, and then investigate homeplace in their own lives and community.

For the part of the activity that does not require AI use, students might make a sound journal of their day, either recording sounds or writing down sounds. What do they hear upon waking? As they spend their morning at home and then travel to school? What does the school day sound like? What are the nighttime sounds of their community? Whose voices are present? What are the sounds of comfort? What sounds cause them distress? The class can then create a collective sound story of their community and ask, What do the sounds of our community show about who we are?

Then, the class can ask an LLM what they might hear in their community. When we asked this question of ChatGPT, we provided a zip code for a community in Baltimore, the city where Marie's university is located. ChatGPT offered up lots of positive soundscapes, including birds chirping from the local park, the sound of school bells and chatter, and the sound of conversation between people out on their front stoops, as well as kids playing baseball and basketball in the park. It also reported sounds of "revitalization noise" which could include hammers and drills, as well as "siren sounds," which it described as follows: "Sirens from ambulances, fire trucks, and police cars are a common part of the urban soundscape in Baltimore, especially in neighborhoods facing crime or health challenges. These sounds can be more frequent in certain parts of 21217, particularly around Sandtown-Winchester."

All of these responses are ripe for teachers to ask students, what do you notice and what do you wonder about the ways ChatGPT described our school neighborhood? It is also an opportunity to compare and contrast what the students identified as important and what the LLM identified as important. Finally, it offers space to explore how LLMs offer one version of what students' community is, and the students may offer similar or competing versions of their community. Teachers can ask students to hypothesize on why the versions may be similar or different. This is also an opportunity for different schools across regions to compare and contrast their sound stories, LLM-generated stories, and their wonders about the technology. Teachers can foster reflective discussion about the role of socioeconomic and cultural contexts and the ways they influence both the students' and the technologies' stories.

Using AI to Make Sense of Math

There are multiple opportunities to use AI in the mathematics classroom. Students may already be inclined to use AI to check or generate answers to mathematics problems. As the teacher, you could provide students with space to check their answers manually or with a traditional calculator, to confirm that AI has provided the correct outputs and is not having a hallucination. This is an important piece, as Jill Barshay wrote in the *Hechinger Report,* because when students trust AI outputs without checking them, they risk memorizing solutions to math problems that are not only incorrect, but also difficult to unlearn, exacerbating confusion around the topic. Barshay also shared a frustrating experience with Khan Academy's Khanmigo chatbot, where she asked for the solution to a sample Algebra 2 question. It took Khanmigo three tries to finally agree with her and produce the correct solution.[32]

Having students participate in an activity where they ask different AI chatbots such as Khanmigo for solutions to problems that they already know the correct solutions to, and having them challenge AI, could help build their agency and confidence. Moreover, this type of learning activity could provide students the chance to practice solving programs, contributing to the accuracy of AI outputs.

Addressing Equity with AI in Math

Teacher Brianna reflects:

To address equity, I've carefully selected tools that are accessible across devices and platforms. For instance, I often use Desmos, a free AI-powered graphing calculator, which levels the playing field for students who might not have access to expensive graphing calculators at home. This tool enables students to visualize complex math concepts and receive immediate feedback, making math more accessible to all learners.

Connecting AI Technologies to Culturally Sustaining STEM Learning

The technology of artificial intelligence inherently uses science, technology, engineering, and mathematics (STEM) to operate. It may feel natural or inevitable that AI is used in K–12 STEM classrooms. STEM activities that use AI technologies can have a two-fold purpose while incorporating culturally relevant, responsive, and sustaining pedagogical practices. This includes concurrently teaching STEM content that connects to the students' cultural capital while preparing students to become critical consumers of AI. As teachers, you can intentionally build and connect students with programs that advance the experience and expertise of STEM.

For example, suppose you are teaching a lesson on innovations in AI, and part of the assignment is for students to learn more about (at the elementary level) or research (at the middle/high school level) pioneers in the field. This lesson could be part of an AI literacy unit, where students would learn about the contributions of individuals whose work has supported advances in AI, similar to how students learn about historical and cultural figures in social studies/history or during cultural heritage days/months in states that allow them (i.e. Black History Month, Latino Heritage Month, Indigenous Peoples Day, Asian/Pacific American Month, etc.). Recognizing the potential limitations and inaccuracies that may result, students can choose a person from a list that they are most interested in, and who may have shared cultural heritages, lived experiences, gender, or other commonalities, and use an AI chatbot such as ChatGPT, Claude, Google Gemini, Microsoft Copilot, and so forth, to find out information about the person and their contributions to AI. You could use the list below as a starting point to provide students with potential options to choose from.

Potential Diverse Pioneers and Contributors to AI

- Isabella Declue, a Latina woman who is a software engineer at Microsoft Copilot. Listed in the Hispanic Executive, among others, as one of "7 Latinos in AI to Watch."[33]
- Laura Montoya, a Latina, a scientist, engineer, and founder of Accel.AI, whose company focused on

lowering the entry to engineering artificial intelligence.[34] Listed in the Hispanic Executive, among others, as one of "7 Latinos in AI to Watch."[35]

- Dr. Fei-Fei Li, a Chinese-American and former Google vice president and Chief Scientist of AI.ML at Google Cloud. Advocates for ethical use of AI, including providing US Senate and Congressional testimonials to policy makers.[36]
- Dr. Ayanna Howard, first woman to lead The Ohio State Engineering College, who has been named in Black Enterprise, TIME Magazine, and as one of the top women in Tech by Forbes. Dr. Howard has contributed over 250 publications to the field, and founded the HumAnS lab which focuses on humanized intelligence.[37] Dr. Howard is also the founder and president of the board of directors of Zyrobotics, which was the recipient of Microsoft's first AI for accessibility grant.

To build on the lesson and provide a chance for students to develop their capacity to be critical consumers of information, and especially information that is a result of an AI output, you can have students then conduct independent research on their pioneer using sources in the library, books, journals, and even by locating video or audio podcast interviews of the person, and compare information. This type of activity taps into students' interests, and connects learning to people with shared lived experiences and cultural assets, within a culturally relevant and responsive lens.

Within a homeplace, the value of uplifting and providing space for self and others necessitates that students be exposed to diverse individuals who share similar cultural and racial lineage, as opposed to only those from the dominant culture. Unfortunately, despite seeing some increases in STEM workforce diversity, an executive report through the

NSF and NCES confirms that white males still dominate the STEM workforce relative to individuals who identify as Asian, Hispanic/Latino, and Black/African Americans, as well as women.[38] We can change this, though! STEM lessons in K–12 can be crafted to teach students about AI and how to use AI in STEM, *while* exposing them to those who are always not equitably represented in STEM spaces who contribute to AI technology development.

We've already seen examples of this in action. The University of California San Francisco (UCSF) has an AI4ALL summer program for high school students which is focused on AI within the biomedicine field, nurturing its diversity and inclusion. The program has specific targets of racial/ethnic groups that have been dramatically underrepresented in AI including Black, Hispanic/Latino, Native American, and young women and those facing/overcoming challenges from low-income backgrounds and future first-generation college students. Tomiko Oskotoshy and colleagues describe one iteration of the UCSF AI4ALL program, sharing the importance of not only ensuring that AI pulls from diverse data sets, but also that the people who are working and leading the field of artificial intelligence are diversity represented.[39] Students, who rarely have previous training on AI or coding, learn about how LLMs and algorithms work, as well as the bias and harms of AI. Students in the program learn about the biases and harms of AI in this summer program through hands-on, experiential experiences. As part of the program, students met with AI role models who were mostly women and underrepresented minorities.[40] At the end of the program, students worked in groups to present research projects which demonstrated their critical thinking around the topics of ethics in AI and science, learning around the development of different models, fluency in using tools such as Python, and their enhanced understanding of AI's applicability through society.

You don't need a fancy program through a university to offer similar experiences in K–12 classrooms, however. There are many ways to ensure that students are aware of the ethical issues related to AI and to support the development of students' consciousness. Through myriad learning activities such as the application examples described in this chapter, you will be able to transition from the harms of AI to providing a homeplace for your students to experience the wonders and joys of AI. In chapter 6, we provide action-oriented steps and content that may be helpful if you do decide to develop such an AI literacy module.

SUMMARY

In the face of dominant narratives, we have seen how marginalized individuals have created a homeplace and refuge from dominant forces of society and AI. Teachers can do the same in their classrooms. We have highlighted some of their work throughout this book, including the work of Dr. Joy Buolamwini (Algorithmic Justice League), Dr. Safiya Noble (UCLA professor and author of *Algorithms of Oppression*), and Dr. Ruha Benjamin (Princeton professor and Ida B. Wells Just Data Lab). School settings are fitting to apply the concept of homeplace, anchoring resistance. Schools have a storied history of institutionalized racism, oppression, and exclusivity that has often positioned white people as the absolute norm, preferred as learners, scholars, and teachers. In spite of this, there is a potential to use classrooms as homeplace in the way that hooks intended, as a place for resistance and liberation.[41] Regarding AI and its use in schools, how we as educators go about the utilization of AI for teaching and learning can and should be in direct opposition to past structures. This includes how schools have functioned since the beginning of their existence. In her invigorating text, *Belong: A Culture Place*, hooks shared her vision of home, wherever that is for each person, to be a place that can be fully enjoyed and one where everyone has a place.[42] While AI in its current state has harms that we have discussed in this book and was not built with all people in mind, our students will still be exposed to AI in this everyday life—for example, through technology tools that are being created specifically as AI tools, as well as existing learning technologies such as the popular questioning ed tech tool, Kahoot, which added AI technologies to the platform.[43] We hope you can see how homeplaces can create sanctuary and rest to allow for dreaming new, just, AI futures. And, your classrooms, especially when using AI, can be just that.

REFLECTION QUESTIONS

After reading this chapter, reflect on the following questions related to culturally relevant, responsive, and sustaining pedagogies.

1. In what ways can I use culturally relevant, responsive, and sustaining pedagogies to support students' use of AI across academic content?
2. How can I establish or nurture a homeplace in a K–12 learning environment for students to pour into as they engage with AI technologies?
3. What, if any, resources are available to you to support your work in creating homeplaces of culturally relevant, responsive, and sustaining pedagogies, and what supports might you need and from whom?

5

Making Good, Necessary Trouble: Resisting and Rebuilding Through Fugitive and Abolitionist Pedagogies

> Do not get lost in a sea of despair. Be hopeful, be optimistic. Our struggle is not the struggle of a day, a week, a month, or a year, it is the struggle of a lifetime. Never, ever be afraid to make some noise and get in good trouble, necessary trouble.
>
> —John Lewis, June 27, 2018, on Twitter

> Get in good trouble, necessary trouble, and help redeem the soul of America.
>
> —John Lewis, March 1, 2020, commemorating the anniversary of Bloody Sunday on the Edmund Pettus Bridge in Selma, Alabama

WHEN JOHN LEWIS ENJOINED citizens to "get in good trouble," he was speaking at the anniversary of Bloody Sunday on the Edmund Pettus Bridge in Selma, Alabama. In that same location, fifty-five years earlier, he was hospitalized after being beaten by police for marching across the bridge during a civil rights protest. When people with power paint activists—especially people of color—as a problem, they have pejoratively called them troublemakers, who are up to no good. Good trouble reclaims and reframes troublemaking. Making good trouble means naming injustice, then engaging in the activism and resistance necessary for a more just world.

John Lewis spent over six decades fighting for human rights and against segregation, working toward justice for all people, especially marginalized humans and in particular Black people.[1] For Congressman Lewis, good and necessary trouble led to forty-five arrests across his lifetime for nonviolent acts of civil disobedience, including one in 2013 at an immigration rally.[2] Lewis carried this ethos with him as he civilly disobeyed unjust laws, even as he worked to craft more equitable laws in the US Congress. Good trouble includes challenging the status quo and calling out racism through word and peaceful action, using the nonviolent mechanisms of activists like Bayard Rustin, Ella Baker, and Dr. Martin Luther King Jr.[3]

In the previous chapter, we provided accessible, culturally relevant, responsive, and sustaining practices that can combat the ways that AI technologies, and the schools in which they are deployed, have historically been spaces of injustice. In this chapter, we use John Lewis' urging toward *good trouble* as a North Star to guide the actions and pedagogies we propose within larger community settings. Fortunately, marginalized educators and students, as well as nonmarginalized allies in school systems, have long histories of teaching toward justice in the midst of oppression. We draw on two of these pedagogical practices, fugitive[4] and abolitionist,[5] to offer learning activities that uplift joyful resisting and rebuilding. Similarly, we suggest learning activities which challenge injustice and work to reclaim AI technologies toward more equitable ends.

FUGITIVE PEDAGOGIES

We are mindful that we write this book in the midst of a highly polarized and politically contentious time. Getting up to good and necessary trouble can feel particularly fraught. States across the US are banning curricula and pedagogical approaches which make even mere mention of race, gender, or sexuality. Moreover, teachers are policed by the state and by extremist parent groups who harness the outrage and virality of social media to cajole, threaten, and pressure teachers and schools into compliance with their demands. In Texas, a principal was placed on leave after school board members accused him of promoting critical race theory. The board refused to renew his contract for the following year.[6] The state of Florida banned the African American Advanced Placement (AP) course in its schools. The College Board, which designs the tests and curriculum for AP courses, responded by removing parts of the curriculum.[7] The Charlotte County school district in Florida demanded teachers remove all books in classrooms and libraries that included any LGBTQ+ characters or themes.[8] Living openly as a trans student or queer teacher can result in physical and emotional violence and the loss of livelihood. Amongst this hate and injustice, we find comfort in the knowledge that marginalized people have always found ways to resist and thrive in oppressive and dangerous conditions.

Fugitive resistance, a powerful and subversive form of good trouble, calls to mind images of enslaved people who self-emancipate, quietly escaping toward liberation even as a network of institutions, from human traffickers to law enforcement to advertisements in local media, were intent on keeping them bound. Stefano Harvey, an American activist and scholar, and Fred Moten, a poet, MacArthur Fellow, and professor of Performance Studies at New York University and Distinguished Professor Emeritus at University of California, Riverside, applied the term of *fugitivity* to the act of teaching, or rather to what becomes possible when we teach *with fugitivity* in spaces that do not wish to hear of justice, abolition, or freedom.[9] It pulls at the seams of oppression, tearing open a small hole, so that the learning on the other side can embody liberation.

Dr. Jarvis R. Givens, a Harvard University professor of education, uses the term *fugitive pedagogies* to describe the historic and current tradition of Black teachers in the US, examining the work of Carter G. Woodson, founder of Black History Month and an educator under Jim Crow. In particular, *fugitive pedagogy* refers to the practices of these teachers as they teach about and for Blackness under a wary and watchful white gaze. From spaces where enslaved children were secretly taught to read and write under penalty of maiming or death, to Black teachers during Jim Crow quietly hiding textbooks containing the full history of the United States under the officially approved textbooks that whitewashed history, fugitive acts occur in the hidden and quiet resistance to oppression. The acts themselves, by their nature, are quiet, but what occurs on the other side of the pedagogy rings loudly of the fullness of freedom. As educators work to address the inequity baked into AI, they may turn to fugitive pedagogies to quietly teach against the harms of the technology.

ABOLITIONIST PEDAGOGY

Dr. Bettina Love, an associate professor of educational theory and practice at the University of Georgia, and a former teacher, powerfully advocates for racial justice in schools through what she terms *abolitionist pedagogy*. As Love writes, "Abolitionist teaching is built on the creativity, imagination, boldness, ingenuity, and rebellious spirit and methods of abolitionists to demand and fight for an education system where all students are thriving, not simply surviving."[10] It is an orientation which requires educators to acknowledge that the policies in the US are racist, discriminatory, and unjust, and name them, and that it is part of our duty as educators and citizens to combine antiracist pedagogy with grassroots organizing in order to abolish structural barriers and rebuild more just systems.

Abolitionist pedagogy draws on Black joy and *freedom dreaming*, which invites us to interrogate the status quo and dream something new and just. For instance, as Love notes, we have been told to accept as "normal" that schools are critically underfunded, that police presence in schools is necessary for safety, that high-stakes standardized tests, which deprofessionalize teachers and whose scores correlate more to race and socioeconomics than learning, are important to "measure" "effective" learning. Freedom dreaming rests in the critique of the historic in order to imagine a beautiful future centered in joy and love. Love contends that "the imaginary world creates new worlds that push democracy, which means politics, schooling, healthcare, citizenship, equal rights, housing, prison, and economics are reimagined for a just world."[11] We would add *technology* to this long list of institutions which can be reimagined.

Love encourages teachers of all grades and subjects to embrace abolitionist pedagogies, highlighting the role of civics in working toward thriving futures for children marginalized by whiteness and power. She suggests that civics education is no longer a space where children learn the fundamentals of doing democracy, including how to speak in public, protest, petition, work collectively with diverse communities to solve social problems, or commit civil disobedience (all acts of *good trouble*). Rather, Love argues, "our students are now taught with the world crumbling around them to pay their taxes, vote, volunteer, and have good character, which is code for comply, comply, comply. Dark children are told that their good character is dependent on how much they obey."[12] She also connects civil disobedience to the technical, reminding us that online petitions and impactful hashtags have helped stir up good trouble. This combination of an antiracist pedagogical approach combined with civic organizing, grounded in freedom dreaming, forms the cornerstone of abolitionist teaching. Abolitionist pedagogy creates spaces to teach *about* injustice embedded in AI and judiciously *with* AI to work toward a more just world.

MAKING GOOD TROUBLE AMID THE DIGITAL: ABOLITION AND FUGITIVITY

We opened the book by discussing the ways AI has automated inequality, and we now offer examples of how to make good trouble, both overtly and with fugitive practice, to work toward abolishing injustice and dreaming new futures. It is probably no accident that Black people, and Black women in particular, have led the work toward digital justice, creating sites to nurture, uplift, and get into good trouble in order to work toward more just AI futures for teachers and students. Hypersurveilled and yet unseen by the same technologies of facial recognition, Black scholars and activists have engaged in powerful acts of collective resistance and good trouble. Indigenous scholars and organizers have similarly reclaimed AI for antiracist and decolonial purposes. The art, creativity, and collective action of several Indigenous scholars use AI to highlight the yoking of land, culture, language, and knowledge. While much of this work is currently occurring outside of school, we share the work of minoritized scholars here to inspire connections to school learning through fugitive and abolitionist pedagogies. Also, much of our students' lives are experienced within society and their communities, as schooling is not delivered in a vacuum. As we examine each act of good trouble, we offer ways this might translate to the classroom when teaching and learning with AI technologies.

Freedom Dreaming Toward Algorithmic and AI Justice

Dr. Joy Buolamwini, the MIT graduate who highlighted the inability of facial recognition software to "see" darker skin, has responded to her encounters with oppressive algorithms by creating the Algorithmic Justice League. This grassroots organization tackles the harms of AI across multiple collective, creative, and clever areas of resistance. Dr. Buolamwini has crafted art and poetry of resistance. Her spoken word poem, "AI, Ain't I a Woman," calls back to Sojourner Truth using images, rhythm, and rhyme to highlight the flat circle of technology and time.[13] Slipping back and forth along the parallels of powerful Black women of the nineteenth century and today, Buolamwini rhymes the ways that AI code cannot see and has no words for their dark skin, faces, and hair, concluding that "no label is worthy of our beauty."[14]

Using Buolamwini's approach as a springboard, teachers could engage students in similar acts of dreaming. Consider sharing Buolamwini's poem and her inspiration as she explored ways that genAI refused to "see" Sojourner Truth. Invite students to ask AI to generate images of a well-known historical figure of color, such as Ella Baker, a powerful freedom fighter of the Civil Rights movement. Ask students to compare this image to historical photographs. Guiding questions could be:

- Do you believe that the image is accurate? Why or why not?
- What do you notice about the image?
- What do you wonder about what the AI chose to highlight and conceal? What do historical photos show?

It may be that students experience anger or frustration if genAI modifies the appearance of activists in ways which represent white and Western standards of beauty and respectability. Students who have darker skin tones may recall their own experiences with technologies which have failed to accurately capture their complexion. It might be that students experience confusion or disbelief. Students with lighter skin tones may not have encountered or considered that technologies could misrepresent humans. As the teacher facilitating these reflective conversations, it will be important to draw upon commitments to openness and criticality, as well as the professional learning and wisdom to ensure a discussion which honors each student's humanity while making space for difference.

To close the activity, you may wish to share Dr. Joy's spoken word poem[15] and invite students to respond to it, or write their own poems. This offers an excellent opportunity to explore art as resistance, and poetry as a means to ask clear and powerful questions about the human experience. This activity might work well in a unit on poetry where the teacher can connect Dr. Joy's poem with other poems of power, protest, and resistance.

Naming injustice is also a part of freedom dreaming. Safiya Noble, MacArthur fellow and author of *Algorithms of Oppression*, was engaging in her own act of homeplace when the domination of the digital broke down the door. Her nieces decided to search the internet for interesting and inspirational images. As we've noted earlier, when Dr. Noble typed "Black girls" into the Google search engine, Google returned hypersexualized and pornographic images of Black girls' bodies to their screens.[16] Galvanized by this uninvited intrusion of the dominant digital into their home, Noble opened a line of research into the artificial intelligence of machine learning algorithms. As a result of this work, Dr. Noble has created several online spaces which foster creativity, critical consciousness, and resistance to the sexism, racism, and oppression magnified by AI. Dr. Noble has also cofounded the Center for Critical Internet Inquiry, which supports research and policy actions toward race and digital justice.

Consider if, in a math class on data visualization, or in a computer science class on algorithmic design, students explored why machine learning results are so skewed. Google has corrected their search since Dr. Noble's callout of their algorithm's results for "Black girls." However, prompting genAI to "show me images of Black hair" produces results that are provocative and generative for discussion and analysis.[17] Figure 5.1 shows the output of what ChatGPT produced for the authors when they inserted the prompt "Show me images of Black hair" in October 2024.

The results show images of hair that is black in color, rather than the many possible hair types of Black people. Black hair is an integral part of a Black body, and Black bodies continue to be a site of political struggle and a canvas for expressions of freedom. It is remarkable to note the way that ChatGPT separated the hair from the head, literally erasing the people to whom the black hair belongs and suggesting hair exists as floating disembodied wigs on the computer screen. Black hair grows across a spectrum of textures, but ChatGPT shared only straight through softly curled examples. There are no examples of tight coils, kinky, or corkscrew hair. Neither are there Black hairstyles including but not limited to afros, dreadlocks, braids, or twists in this genAI-crafted response.

Figure 5.1 October 2024 ChatGPT results for prompt "show me images of Black hair"

ChatGPT erased race and gender from the search results for Black hair, and this is merely one example of AI platforms' tendency to erase or overlook results that reflect the full scope and diversity of humanity. When conducting lessons that incorporate such biased results from ChatGPT or other platforms, teachers might start by asking students what they notice and what they wonder about genAI produced images. Then, they can take this conversation further by asking students to consider what data ChatGPT is trained on. Finally, the teacher and students can share how they might change the training data of AI. It's also powerful to ask students what we give up when we ask ChatGPT to show us Black hair, instead of talking to friends, family, and community. Black barber shops and hair salons are notable spaces for exchange of community wisdom and replication of culture. The homeplace, to refer to our work in the last chapter, is a nurturing space to learn about identity. What does a student give up when they ask a biased algorithm questions of identity instead of turning to a site of homeplace or community? Can genAI, a technology which is uncannily adept at socializing and sounding human, ever offer a digital analog to the rich sociocultural geographies of a community? And should it?

Similarly ripe for discussion are simple prompts like "show me an image of a teacher" and "show me an image of a ballerina." When we prompted it, ChatGPT showed us a young, bearded, white man standing at the back of his classroom, but facing the viewer. Oddly, he is at a podium with a pen, but he faces away from the students. The students sit in neat rows of desks behind him, with their backs to us and to him. There is one Black student in the class, and the other students appear white. The image of the ballerina depicts a tall and thin white woman with her light brown hair in a bun. She wears a white leotard and skirt, and has her arms gracefully outstretched.

In response to these images, teachers could ask students to dream a new school image or Black hair or ballerina for ChatGPT to create. For a learning activity, create a hands-on AI lab experience where students run experiments to see how many times they have to reprompt the AI before it gives them the wide array of natural and protective hairstyles that Black people wear. On a lab sheet, students jot down the assumptions present in these images and which of those assumptions they would like to reject and resist. Finally, students will reflect and share any frustrations or disappointments to OpenAI, the makers of ChatGPT.

Dr. Tiera Tanksley, a scholar based out of UCLA who investigates race, technology, and education, has created space for future dreaming through her project, Race, Activism, & Digital Wellness. Out of that work she organized a summer computer science course for teens, the Race, Abolition, and AI Program. Developed during the summer of 2020, after the murder of George Floyd, Dr. Tanksley's workshop offered an intentional refuge from the bombardment of online images of violence against Black bodies, amplified by algorithms which profit from oppression and objectification. On the program's website, Dr. Tanksley's describes the work as

> a critical race tech program: it is focused on developing the sociological and computational skills to allow teens to understand how race and technology intersect so that they can be empowered to navigate and eventually redesign technologies in ways that uplift, rather than harm, people of color. The program focuses explicitly on Black identities, cultural experiences, and funds of knowledge, and the kinds of algorithmic anti-Blackness that scholar Dr. Ruha Benjamin calls "the new Jim Code."[18]

Over the years, the workshop has also become a site of resistance and reimagination. Recently, students investigated why the class robot, Moxie, would respond to questions and interests around topics like dinosaurs, but when asked about Black hair or Black history, Moxie would respond, "Let's do something more fun, that sounds like a sad topic."[19] With the support and guidance of Dr. Tanksley, the students proposed creating a different robot whom they named Jordan. The students identified which race-conscious data should be used to train Jordan, and they proposed ways to design racially just algorithms to program Jordan.

It's disturbing to consider that the AI assumed Blackness is a "sad topic," and it was best to shy away from teaching about Blackness. First, Black hair and Black history are filled with instances of joy, pride, and power, and equating Blackness with sadness is to diminish and degrade Black people. As bell hooks noted when she coined the term homeplace, living joyfully is a powerful act of resistance against oppression. Furthermore, there are parts of Black history (like all histories) that include personal and collective acts of violence and racism, and teaching hard history is fundamental to justice. Hard histories can be taught from early childhood using age-appropriate pedagogies, and should not only be a topic reserved for older students.[20] An AI bot deflecting or erasing these histories only reinforces stereotypes and perpetuates half-truths of the past.

Moreover, this "glitch" in Moxie, wherein it found Blackness to be a "sad topic," promotes a white fragility mind-set. This causes us to wonder, what else might AI consider to be too "sad" to engage with? We encourage teachers and students to work together to find the edges of AI's tolerance for what hard histories or marginalized identities feel too "unsafe" for it to teach. For instance, in an English class where students are reading stories, poems, or biographies that include themes of identity, students might ask a genAI model about each of these themes. With the teacher, students might discuss what topics the AI seems to embrace, and those which it may use more hesitant language, or require more prompts, to address.

Dr. Ruha Benjamin, professor of African Studies at Princeton, MacArthur fellow, and author of several books, including *Race After Technology: Abolitionist Tools for the New Jim Code*, has also used her scholarship to generate a space for learning and new imaginings through the Ida B. Wells Just Data Lab at Princeton. The lab "brings together students, educators, activists, and artists to develop a critical and creative approach to data conception, production, and circulation. Our aim is to rethink and retool the relationship between stories and statistics, power and technology, data and justice."[21] The students at the lab engage in community partnership and research to understand issues of data and justice. The students use art, imagination, and research to interrogate data injustices and propose alternative futures.

One of the powerful projects to come out of the Just Data Lab is student crafted zines. Zines have a long history as self-published underground media, originally photocopied and, in the digital age, sometimes posted online as webzines. Zines offer counternarratives, counterculture ideas, and a DIY, punk ethos. The students at the lab published their findings on data and policing, health care, education, and other institutions as online zines that can be accessed and shared through the data lab website. In the classroom, teachers can encourage students to develop their own zines around topics of justice and AI. Since zines often act as a primary source based on someone's personal experience, students can choose a topic relevant to their own lives and identities.

Michael Running Wolf, founder of Indigenous AI, envisions using AI to elevate indigenous knowledge without allowing it to be exploited. Running Wolf is Northern Cheyenne, Blackfeet, and Lakota. He is working on developing a walled garden approach to AI data, rather than an open access approach. Many geographic sites need to be preserved, but also protected. He notes that certain plants, important to Indigenous medicine, are threatened by climate change. He would like to create open access databases that track climate change and its effect on the environment, and then walled garden databases that note where particular and threatened plants are growing. He is cautious about data, but sees it as an opportunity:

> People say, "Data is the new oil" and I think that's apt. Like oil, the extraction of data can be harmful to the local environment and the world. Companies take data into their databases and it becomes proprietary information, and then communities lose access to it. They lose the relationship to their own information—be it geographic or voice data. We need to change the paradigm to say that data is human.[22]

Dream with your students about parts of their culture which they would like to see preserved, amplified, and protected. Is there a way to design and develop a walled garden approach for their language, music, history, food, or family? If not, how might they design something that offers the power of genAI but uses an approach like the carefully curated collection that Running Wolf seeks to protect?

Civic Action for Justice in AI

Dr. Buolamwini's good trouble extends in other directions as well. She has galvanized a grassroots collective of residents in a Brooklyn apartment building who were subjected to facial recognition technology in order to enter their homes. Together, they worked to resist the company and compel the apartment complex to remove the facial recognition system surveilling them as they entered and exited their homes. The Netflix documentary *Coded Bias* follows Buolamwini as she works alongside the residents to fight against the algorithmic injustices forced upon them.

Following that action, the Algorithmic Justice League has created the Community Reporting of Algorithmic System Harms (CRASH) project.[23] The CRASH project brings people who have been harmed by algorithmic oppression together in community and iterates solutions to the harms. Redressing the harms may involve resisting the technologies as well as engaging in ways to build more just AI systems.

The Algorithmic Justice League also employs education to work toward more just AI futures. They partner with drag queens to offer workshops which explore gender, identity, and the way that facial algorithms read (drag pun!) a face. They host educational sessions where participants play with gender and drag makeup to outfox surveillance software, consider what it means to be read by artificial intelligence, and then learn how to take collective actions to stop artificial intelligence abuses.[24]

Dr. Buolamwini has also engaged in what may be considered more traditional forms of participation in the democratic process. She has testified before the US Congress regarding the harms of artificial intelligence. She has lobbied internationally at Davos' annual meeting of the World Economic Forum. She has written op-eds and policy pieces in mainstream media, and she continues to research and write about the intersection of race, gender, and AI.

With support of teachers, students may wish to start their own version of an Algorithmic Justice League at school. In social studies classes, or in an after school club, students could investigate a particular question around AI and the school or community. It may be as local as "what happens when teachers use generative AI to give feedback to students at our school?" or "how is our school using AI based programs to keep track of students?" Given what we already know about encoded bias, neither of these questions can be fully answered without considering the disproportionate harms of algorithms on already vulnerable students.

A powerful example of someone asking these questions and making good trouble is Marika Pfefferkorn, who cofounded the Twin Cities Innovation Alliance with Aasim Shabazz. The mission of their organization is

> to build and develop a critical mass of diverse, highly engaged residents, policy makers, and entrepreneurs, made up of minorities and people of color traditionally identified as the end users and consumers of innovation and design, and transforming them into the purveyors and beneficiaries. This will benefit all communities across the nation and our world. We exchange learnings while adapting and evolving our collective work.[25]

In seeking to ensure people of color are subject, not object, they host multiple actions and opportunities for empowering agency in the Twin Cities. Through Pfefferkorn's Midwest Center for School Transformation, she and other community members realized that some school systems in the region had adopted the AI software Gaggle, which tracks student typing and flags certain words, without any community input. The software was flagging LGBTQIA+ students and outing them to their teachers and families. With the community, they argued that this surveillance software was exacerbating the school-to-prison pipeline, criminalizing youth. When the state faced a budget crisis, Pfefferkorn and her fellow activists were able to convince the state that Gaggle was a waste of resources, and Minnesota did not renew the contract.

In a powerful example of collective action, the Detroit Community Technology Project works toward equitable digital futures in Detroit and in partnership with other cities across the US.[26] They have fought for internet access in underserved neighborhoods, but instead of treating the technology of the internet as an unencumbered good, they partner the technology with a digital literacy initiative. Drawing on the knowledge of the community, members of the community are designated as *digital stewards* who host workshops, advisory councils, and participatory design projects to help ensure all members of the community can confidently access the internet.

In what ways can students in schools be digital stewards of AI? Could your school create its own advisory council of community members and students who become the local stewards of both AI knowledge and community knowledge and preservation? These students can mentor fellow students, teachers, and members of the community in how to use AI in thoughtful and confident ways.

The Detroit Community Technology Project has also challenged the ways that surveillance technologies disproportionately harm communities of color. In January 2016, the Detroit Police Department initiated Project Green Light. Project Green Light links cameras at local businesses to police headquarters, and uses facial recognition software to attempt to connect the faces of the people the camera thinks it sees to criminal activity. The Detroit Community Technology Project, in coalition with other civil rights organizations, vigorously opposed the Project Green Light. They initiated petitions and urged citizens to contact their state representatives to pass privacy bills in Michigan.[27] They rallied attendance at Detroit Police Department meetings and press conferences. Through community workshops and newsletters, they educated on the difference between "safe" communities and "secure" communities. Secure communities, they point out, require the carceral logics of surveillance and policing, augmented by technology. Instead, The Detroit Community Technology Project dreamed a new vision for safety in their community, calling for "green chairs instead of green lights." Young people walking to school invited the elders of the community to sit in green chairs, to be present as the children walked to and from school. Green chairs on front porches mean something particular and special when someone chooses to sit in them. It is a space for participation and for care, for active attention to the community from people who know the faces of those walking past—without having to query a failed algorithm to identify each other.[28]

Teachers and students can similarly resist surveillance AI in schools by creating their own equivalents of "green chairs." What if, instead of swipe ID cards or video surveillance to track students' whereabouts, community members were present in the school throughout the day, comfortably ensconced in places throughout the school building—perhaps on sofas or by a table with water and snacks, offering little mini-homeplaces wherein students could stop, visit, and be encouraged to travel safely to their next learning experience. This vision might seem like a far-off dream, but it's a dream worth not just striving for, but working toward.

Fugitive Acts

While many of the examples and suggested activities above include direct action and discussion of injustice, quieter everyday acts of resistance also serve to work toward a more just implementation of AI in schools. Intentionally slow adoption of a harmful surveillance product, a quiet refusal to implement a technology, or offering analog or less harmful technologies as a substitution are powerful ways to prevent technology companies from further automation of inequality.

For instance, in some schools, teachers and students may be required to use certain programs (e.g., iReady for math and reading skills) for a certain amount of time each day. In chapter 2, we analyzed the ways that overreliance on so-called "personalized learning" software dehumanizes students, reinforces the normative status quo, further deprofessionalizes teachers, attempts to separate an individual student from the complex systems in which they live and learn, applies opaque algorithms to student learning, scrapes student data, and has a long, almost one-hundred-year history of hype, hope, and disappointment in schools. In our work with teachers, they have expressed frustration at the ways iReady and other machine learning AI programs become a required crutch for "teaching" math and reading, especially in chronically underfunded schools. They cannot see individual student answers, only iReady's algorithmic calculation report of student "success" in the gamified program. Regardless, the schools rely on iReady data to make decisions about instruction and further iReady remediation of skills. In our work with students, they report that they increasingly dislike math when they are forced to do repetitive iReady math problems to remediate their math skills. Regardless, school systems continue to purchase the software and implement required screen time for children to use iReady.

Good trouble and fugitive pedagogies inherently require some level of risk, and we are mindful that teachers balance many competing and complex needs as they navigate their work. Thus when we recommend these fugitive pedagogies to resist iReady and other mandated personalized learning softwares, we invite teachers to weigh the potential risks and rewards to their students. This is a place to lean into critical consciousness and the rebellious spirit of good trouble. Students we work with report that they hack iReady by logging into the software and leaving it open on the computer, accumulating seeming time on task, but without feeding the iReady data. One possible fugitive pedagogy for refusing mandated and uncritical use of AI technologies is to engage students in a discussion (rather than immediately punishing students) for their own hacks to iReady. Students also report intentionally answering incorrectly in order to skew data, forcing iReady to read them as incapable, and offering them easier problems. Instead of immediately chastising students and forcing compliance, this opens up space for discussion about the students' reasons for resisting, their clever resistance tactics, the potential impacts on their education, and conversations about other ways to build math and reading skills outside of iReady.

If teachers feel inspired by the tactics of their students, they may consider their own resistance. Perhaps as a class, teachers and students could critically examine iReady and its purpose in the classroom. What kind of learning is gained and lost through the use or misuse of iReady? What do students learn about citizenship, compliance, and democracy through this? We are mindful that different districts and administrations may have divergent approaches to policy and practice. Fugitivity inherently contains within it a rebellious spirit. We also know that folks need their livelihoods. Thus, we are not offering these activities as "must-dos" but rather "may dos," within the confines, context, and ability of each teacher's complicated professional environment.

Another fugitive approach to using required AI technologies could be to review the default settings with students. Together, open up the settings and review each setting as a class. Invite students to turn off settings which collect, surveil, or force default to choices which benefit the company, not the child. Teachers we work with have hosted parent information nights about technology, and they do similar activities, including a family review of the permissions of school software, in order to make clear what data is collected, how families can opt out, and how families can express their viewpoints about the technology to the school system and the school board.

Young people are engaging in their own acts of refusal, creating *Luddite Clubs* which meet to engage in analog activities and interactions.[29] The term Luddite refers to an early nineteenth century movement of English master weavers whose knowledge, craftsmanship, and livelihoods were being replaced by early industrial machines. The weavers were not anti-technology; rather, they were opposed to the way that budding capitalists were relocating the art of weaving from the home to a factory, degrading quality of life and co-opting the weavers' skills.[30]

Some students, inspired by the Luddites, have given up their smartphones and use flip phones instead. They recognized themselves that they were unduly influenced by the AI of social media algorithms and the lure of the small screen, and so they decided to refuse to use their smartphones. An unexpected challenge for the students was the constant use of phones to facilitate access to school-mannered technology. They often needed an app or two-factor authentication for school projects that they were unable to access without a smartphone. Even applying to colleges was difficult without having the accessibility of ever-present email, text verifications, and apps required for access to different application portals.

Teachers may help students who choose to refuse harmful technology by allowing students to opt out without penalty. If a student decides that an AI technology is too invasive, too harmful to the environment, too dangerous to trans or queer or Black or Indigenous people or other marginalized folks, then a teacher can help that student uphold their resistance. We can work with students to find workarounds, so that students may opt out of technology but still effectively learn. This may include standing in solidarity with the student and letting the administration know you want to find a way to allow the student to opt out of some technology, but still use other tech. To that end, another fugitive pedagogy involves asking the question, "How will this learning activity be different if we use AI and if we don't use AI?" and "What changes about learning if we use AI for this activity and if we don't?"

Another fugitive pedagogy is to quietly retrain, or at least aim to disrupt, the racist and bigoted data that AI consumes. When Reddit users learned that OpenAI was scraping Reddit posts to feed its algorithms, the Redditors (people who use Reddit) began posting humorous and obviously fake posts about cities, people, and events. Another option to consider with students is whether entering misleading data into a racist machine is a virtuous act of throwing sand into the gears of the machine. In other words, consider whether this is an act in the vein of civil disobedience attempting to disrupt embedded bias and harnessing the rebellious spirit Bettina Love encourages, or, might students argue, is it ethically wrong to intentionally mislead the technology? We suggest that a little joyful act of clever rebellion is in line with the type of civic action for which Love advocates.

Finally, teachers may teach *about* acts of resistance toward AI in the world. For instance, when learning about acts of political dissent in social studies classes, consider teaching students about protesters in San Francisco who immobilize autonomous driving cars by placing a traffic cone on its hood.[31] The car can no longer "see," and therefore it cannot work. Smart cars, especially given faulty facial recognition systems which fail to see darker skinned individuals, and the tendency of the cars to record everything occurring around them, are particularly dangerous to people of color.[32] Teachers can also share the ways that protesters in Hong Kong shone laser pointers at police surveillance cameras to disrupt the facial recognition AI being used to identify and jail them.[33] In all of these acts are the lessons of good trouble, and of resistance and refusal, that can open possibilities for students to reject narratives of AI for efficiency and instead consider AI for justice.

SUMMARY

Each of these examples of good trouble rests on the power of the collective and a commitment to abolition. Abolition is not simply a tearing down; it is a reimagining and rebuilding as well. From green chairs instead of green lights of surveillance, to Indigenous languages for the future in the hands of the people to whom the words belong, to wild and unruly counterculture digital zines exposing the raw underbelly of power, we find inspiration in the good trouble.

REFLECTION QUESTIONS

After reading this chapter, reflect on the following questions related to the relationship of good trouble, fugitive pedagogies, and abolitionist pedagogies.

1. What is your comfort level with making good trouble in your classroom or with your students? What do you think influences that level of comfort or discomfort?

2. What is the difference between teaching *about* AI and teaching *with* AI? When should we be doing each?
3. What real world examples in this chapter resonated with you? How can you modify or adapt these examples to the content you teach?

6

Toward JustAI: Taking Personal, Professional, Pedagogical, and Participatory Action

> All too often, when we see injustices, both great and small, we think, That's terrible, but we do nothing. We say nothing. We let other people fight their own battles. We remain silent because silence is easier. *Qui tacet consentire videtur* is Latin for "Silence gives consent." When we say nothing, when we do nothing, we are consenting to these trespasses against us.
>
> —Roxane Gay, *Bad Feminist*

ABOLITIONIST APPROACHES TO INSTRUCTION require educators to engage in actions for a more just world inside and outside of the classroom. In this final chapter of the book, we offer action items to make change toward more just AI. We have developed four areas for enacting change that are inspired by the work of Patricia Hill Collins, who wrote, "People experience and resist oppression on three levels: the level of personal biography; the group or community level of the cultural context created by race, class, and gender; and the systemic level of social institutions. Black feminist thought emphasizes all three levels as sites of domination and as potential sites of resistance."[1] Thus, we offer the four categories of the personal, the pedagogical, the professional, and the participatory (or collective). In each of these four domains we provide clear and actionable examples you can take to make change toward a more just use of AI.

TAKING PERSONAL ACTIONS

As we work toward justice-centered use of AI in K–12 classrooms, we should start with reflecting on the personal actions we can take in our lives. Why? Because the way we operate in our personal lives influences aspects of our teaching. Think back to chapter 3's discussion on how mind-sets influence our approaches to AI. Remember how teachers Gio, Ari, and Kel's thoughts, attitudes, and beliefs influenced how they used AI in their respective classrooms. In a similar vein, the personal actions we take toward AI engagement have impacts on how we move forward with using it in our profession.

Personal Action 1: Plan and Protect Your Privacy

We have discussed the potential harms of AI in how data is collected, harvested, and distributed. Consider the ways in which you protect your own data, when and where you share your data, and how that data may be used to influence your shopping behaviors, thoughts on societal topics, and even how you approach teaching. This may take some time, but you can start by reviewing your privacy and default settings for every application you have on your mobile devices, such as your cell phone or tablet. The National Cybersecurity Alliance has a sizeable list with links to various websites where personal data is stored, including e-commerce, music, mobile banking, online conferencing, email and voice communication, online dating, health applications, photo and video sharing, food delivery services, rideshare/scooter rental services, mobile/location services, travel, search engines, social networks, streaming platforms, web browsers, and other miscellaneous sites.[2] As you work on personal action 1, go through the list and click on each link that is relevant to the websites and applications you use. Each link will take you to the company's corresponding privacy page. From there, you can modify your settings according to your personal preferences, based on how comfortable you are with aspects of your data (such as name, birthdate, location, or the tracking of what websites are visited and when) being accessible to the apps and website you use. This habit from your personal life has the potential to follow into your use of AI and ed tech in your classrooms—meaning, the actions in your personal life will translate into the pedagogical actions you take in your classroom. And, you will be well informed and well versed at protecting the privacy and data settings within these digital tools and websites.

Personal Action 2: Investigate and Influence Your Digital Footprint

Beyond our mobile devices' privacy settings, it's important to examine your own search engine usage, social technologies, and habits. We encourage you to listen to New York Public Radio's Privacy Paradox (on the Note to Self podcast) and complete their five-day challenge, a series of mini-podcasts and newsletters focused on how you can take back control of your digital identity and personal information online. Once you sign up[3], you will receive an email with the link to the daily episode and corresponding newsletter. As their website states, "We'll send you 5 newsletters. Each includes tips and a short podcast explaining the science, psychology, and tech behind that day's challenge." Each day, there are topics surrounding the ways in which your data is tracked and distributed throughout online spaces, encouraging you to change your online behaviors to better protect your digital footprint. Day 1, "What Your Phone Knows," looks at the metadata that your smartphone collects and why it is important. Day 2, "The Search for Your Identity," explains how algorithms see us in order to market to us. Day 3, "Something to Hide," encourages us to take back our data and how it is used. Day 4, "Fifteen Minutes of Anonymity," discusses the importance of separating self from online. Day 5, "Your Personal Terms of Service," is focused on deciding what conditions are acceptable to you for being safe and healthy while online.[4]

After completing the Privacy Paradox five-day challenge, it may be helpful to engage in a digital fast. This can be challenging. This is a time to disconnect from technology and be still. A main element of a digital fast is dedicating a certain amount of time each week, or a certain day during each month, to be 100 percent free of digital devices. It may be useful to schedule the digital fast for accountability purposes, and write down your schedule in a physical calendar. Journaling during the periodic digital fast can help you center yourself as you continue to negotiate your digital identity and take personal actions to project your digital footprint. This type of personal action may positively spill over into your classrooms as well, saving the use of AI for intentionally pedagogical uses where it makes sense to use AI to create justice-centered learning opportunities for students.

Personal Action 3: Review and Redirect Search Engines and Habits

Our digital footprint is influenced heavily by our online search behaviors. What we search for in search engines such as Google, Yahoo, and Bing provides data for developers and businesses to glean our interests and dislikes. This is also data that AI technologies will pull from. A personal action you can take as you work toward just AI is to pull up your search history from Google, for example. Google provides simple directions to do so, which are linked in endnote 5.[5] Review your data and compare your maps, photos, emails, search history, YouTube videos. Reflect on these questions: What does Google know about me? and How do I feel? Then, change your settings and your search engine. Consider using a search engine like DuckDuckGo, which turns off tracking. The 2023 CNET article, "5 Reasons You Should Use DuckDuckGo Instead of Google," notes that

DuckDuckGo's search engine stops trackers from spying, shows fewer ads, may create faster loading of websites, and does not store search history, which in turn provides search results that are not influenced by browsing history.[6] If students see you modeling use of DuckDuckGo instead of the typical Google search, they may in turn be less likely to instantly Google for information. These are behaviors consistent with being a good digital citizen, aligned with information literacy, and have the potential to influence the ways in which students understand AI-generated information.

Personal Action 4: Understand and Utilize Related Laws

You may be familiar with federal laws and policies surrounding technology and education. For example, in your work as an educator, you have likely read about the Family Educational Rights and Privacy Act (FERPA), a law that protects the privacy of student records and educational information. To a lesser extent, you may be familiar with the Children's Online Privacy Protection Act (COPPA), a law that provides parents with protections on data that websites can collect from their children under age thirteen, or the Child Internet Protection Act (CIPA), which requires schools and libraries to filter and block harmful content from student access. All of these laws regulate information and technology, and serve to protect children in online spaces. According to the National Conference of State Legislators, forty-five states, along with Washington, DC, Puerto Rico, and the Virgin Islands, have enacted legislation or adopted resolutions related to AI.[7] While it may feel daunting, it is important to be aware of relevant technology and artificial intelligence policies, laws, and regulations that are being developed and enacted in your state and at the federal level. To get started, go to the National Conference of State Legislators (NCSL) Artificial Intelligence 2024 Legislation page (www.ncsl.org/technology-and-communication/artificial-intelligence-2024-legislation) to find out about laws in the state in which you teach, so you can be informed when you participate in conversations with your school administration on the topic.

TAKING PEDAGOGICAL ACTIONS

Throughout this book we have detailed the harms of AI, how to shift our mind-sets toward just AI, and pedagogical strategies to use AI in ways that bring joy to your students. Now is the time to deploy your knowledge and strategies toward pedagogical action.

Pedagogical Action 1: Conduct a Technoethical/Technoskeptical Audit

One such action is to evaluate any and all ed tech tools you use in the classroom. More specifically, look for ways that ed tech tools include AI components, and how the AI is being used. As part of teaching students about responsible and ethical use of AI, engage in a technoethical or technoskeptical audit of technology tools that you use in your classroom that include AI components. To do this, partner with students to ask technoskeptical questions when evaluating AI tools that are available to your class. This exercise will provide a chance to take a pause and consider technology before adoption and use. Some technoskeptical questions that can guide this pedagogical action include: What does society give up for the benefits of this technology?, In what ways, if any, will using the technology tools reinforce harm?, and What are some of the intended and unintended consequences of using the technology tool? You can also ask questions which help uncover the ethics of a technology. This includes questions like: Are the environmental resources for this technology ethically sourced?, What are the labor practices to support this technology?, and Is the data for this technology ethically sourced? We recognize that these are big questions, without immediate answers. As such, part of the purpose of the audit is to research and engage in inquiry together with students to uncover the answers. These questions will lead to a larger discussion with students, and may curb some of the automaticity that is associated with immediately using a technology tool without thinking about the ramifications.

Pedagogical Action 2: Solidify a JustAI Policy for Students and Yourself

Identify and review your school's acceptable use policy to determine what parameters there are regarding AI use for students. Then, in alignment with your school district's policy, solidify your own AI policy for your students and for yourself. Your policy may not be the same as the school's policy, but it should be consistent with it for transparency and continuity. If your policy differs, have a discussion with your administrator about how to reconcile it, and advocate for and explain why your policy is written to support and protect students as they use AI technologies. As you craft your policy, decide how you will use AI to create content, engage learners, and assess learning. Align your AI policy with all that you know about ethical, responsible, and just AI. You may want to broaden your AI policy to technology tools in general—for example, including the use of DuckDuckGo as the search engine of choice. There is no perfect policy. Each school has distinct makeup, needs, and resources, but the content throughout this book can support your drafting of your own AI policy. One overarching question to consider after you have written the first draft of your AI policy is: "How does my AI policy support the potential for joyful experiences for all students when using AI technologies in my classroom?" Be mindful of how students may interact with AI at home. Having an intentional and clear JustAI policy for your classrooms will be helpful as you work toward using AI for justice and joy. Stay nimble and flexible, establishing your JustAI policy as a working document that will go through iterations as AI technologies continue to evolve and become more widely available to students.

Pedagogical Action 3: Support Students in Producing a JustAI PSA for Teaching

It's important for students to have agency and buy-in when engaging with AI technologies, and to have the opportunity to share their learning with a wider audience. Have students create a short thirty to sixty second PSA describing how AI should be used ethically and responsibly for teaching and learning. Students can lean into the experiences they will gain with evaluating AI tools and conducting a technoethical/technoskeptical audit, as well as from engaging with AI tools in ways that align with your own AI policy. This way, students' communities, families, and other students in the school and district can learn about how to use AI in justice-centered ways from their peers. It can be more powerful for students to hear from the voices of their fellow students rather than from a stranger or even an adult teacher. This pedagogical action also supports developing students' public speaking skills and creative outputs.

TAKING PROFESSIONAL ACTIONS

As educators, we hold power in our professional spaces. We are experts in education and can use our wisdom of practice and professional learning to work with our fellow professionals to effect change in our schools. The following actions leverage the knowledge and spaces of professional education practice, including school boards, school improvement teams, professional learning networks, and the informal spaces of professional conversation in faculty rooms and hallways.

Professional Action 1: Review Existing AI Frameworks for Commitments to Justice

The first professional action recommendation builds on the previous personal and pedagogical actions. If your school or district is planning to introduce AI tools or create policy around AI, explore and compare existing AI frameworks, which look for commitments to justice. Many frameworks outline fair use policies, particularly around ethics and possibilities for misrepresenting student work, but few examine issues of data justice, environmental justice, or pedagogical justice. One framework that we recommend as a starting point for developing your district- or school-wide policy is the Kapor Foundation's *Responsible AI and Tech Justice: A Guide for K12 Education*. The framework describes itself as "A guide designed for K-12 educators and students to support the critical interrogation of artificial intelligence and its implications on individuals, community, and the world."[8] It begins from a place of ethics, justice, and criticality, stating: "While it is critical to delineate guidance for how teachers, students, and schools use AI tools in the advancement of education, it is equally important to prioritize how students and educators interrogate ethics, equity, and justice in the creation, deployment, and utilization of AI technologies as a core component of a robust K–12 education."[9] By ensuring that justice and ethics are equally as important as content and innovation, the framework builds out reflective questions and opportunities for educators to work with students toward just approaches to AI. Moreover, the framework was developed in concert with critical AI scholars including many of those we've cited in this book, such as Drs. Safiya Noble, Emily Bender, and Chris Gilliard, and the coauthor of this book, Marie.

Professional Action 2: Lobby School Boards

Teachers can lobby the school board to take action to argue for more just implementation of AI policies in schools. To do so, teachers can work alongside other professionals and with families and community. We have worked with computer science teachers who have collaborated with students and families as citizen scientists to gather data on ed tech and AI programs that their schools have purchased. For instance, one teacher and her students compared the data privacy of students who could only use school-provided Wi-Fi with students who could use their family Wi-Fi at home. In this district, students who could not afford

Wi-Fi were given school Wi-Fi hotspots in order to access the internet at home. While this decreased the digital access divide, the school-supported Wi-Fi was surveilled and limited in ways which could harm minoritized students.

With colleagues and the community, the teacher examined maps of her district, which overlaid maps of poverty with maps of race. She identified the ways that students who received the school Wi-Fi hotspots intersected with majority Black student populations. With her students, she collected data on how student internet access was surveilled at school and at home. They identified which topics and websites were set as off limits. Then she worked with the community to present her findings at the school board meeting to demonstrate that school-based Wi-Fi hotspots, while well intended, discriminated against Black students in her district.

Professional Action 3: Host a Teach-In on AI

Many schools host tech nights, art evenings, and other events which highlight the work of students and the school. We encourage schools to host a teach-in for families on AI. Teach-ins are rooted in practical, action-oriented justice work. Students can do their own investigations and lead presentations on what algorithms are, how they work, how programmers "feed" AI and where the data comes from, the environmental impacts of AI, and data privacy. These roundtable presentations can also include a table for community impacts. Depending on the location of the school, the community may already be experiencing impacts of environmental degradation for data centers or surveillance from facial recognition. At these tables, connect community members with organizations already doing the work of standing up to injustice. At other tables, share the work of positive examples of AI being used to preserve language and culture, and share projects of student work with AI. The goal of the teach-in is to more deeply understand the complexity and nuance of generative AI in schools and society.

Professional Action 4: Facilitate a Book Study or Movie Night

Faculty book studies through professional learning communities are a powerful way to develop technoskeptical approaches and critical consciousness. Organize a book series with a group of faculty, perhaps a grade-level or content-level team, to read and discuss the books which influenced *this* book. For instance, the teachers could choose to do a series on critical pedagogies including Django Paris's book *Culturally Sustaining Pedagogies: Teaching and Learning for Justice in a Changing World,* Bettina Love's book *We Want to Do More Than Survive: Abolitionist Teaching and the Pursuit of Educational Freedom,* and Jarvis Givens' book *Fugitive Pedagogy: Carter G. Woodson and the Art of Black Teaching.*

Faculty can also work to develop technoskeptical mind-sets through joining existing book clubs who read books about technology and education. The Civics of Technology (www.civicsoftechnology.org) project hosts a monthly book club for educators on Zoom featuring different technology and education books. Teachers may also watch and discuss films and interviews which help them better understand AI and its intersection with society. We recommend the *Coded Bias* documentary on Netflix that follows Joy Buolamwini's scholarship and subsequent activism toward more just AI use in society.

Professional Action 5: Partner with the School Improvement Team

One effective way to make change in your professional space is by influencing policy at the school level. If your school has a data team or school improvement team, this is a place where you can make recommendations for policy and practice in your school. You might recommend that the school improvement team analyze data around ed tech products that use AI. Work to center just and ethical uses of AI, as much or even more than innovative possibilities of AI products.

Professional Action 6: Speak Up and Out in Professional Spaces

One of the simplest yet sometimes most challenging actions is to speak up and speak out in our professional spaces to address techno-optimism and encoded bias in language and practice. When in conversation with peers, we can implement critical consciousness and technoskeptical mind-sets, disrupting the biased speech and techno-optimism so prevalent in the ways that we inadvertently discuss education technologies.

TAKING PARTICIPATORY (COLLECTIVE) ACTIONS

Change in personal, pedagogical, and professional spaces is necessary and important. However, it is the actions of the collective which make institutional change. Finding like-minded individuals committed to working toward the common good, many whose organizations have already built effective infrastructure for change, is a powerful way to participate in collective actions. Below, we make recommendations for spaces and actions which center on technology and justice. Like all of our recommendations, these vary in scale and intensity. Some may be easier or simpler to enact, and others may take more time, commitment, or potential risk.

Participatory Action for Justice 1: Join a Union or Teacher Association

Unions and teacher associations are designed to leverage the power of the collective in education spaces. The power of unions can be context-specific—for instance, in some states or districts, collective bargaining and striking rights are limited. However, these associations still exist as a collective power for education. Moreover, certain teachers' unions, such as the BMORE (Baltimore Movement of Rank and File Educators) Caucus, active in the Baltimore City schools through 2022, have created agendas which intentionally center bargaining around issues of social justice for Baltimore city school students.[10]

After joining your union or association, consider running as a representative from your school to the association. At the representative meetings, bring issues of AI justice to the association. Associations and unions are one effective way to lean into the power of the collective to bring JustAI to the fore.

Participatory Action for Justice 2: Join a Technology Collective

Other collectives include national and community organizations which center technology, justice, and democracy. The Center for Democracy and Technology offers working groups and practical guides for educators and citizens (cdt.org/inventory-of-civic-tech-practitioner-guidance/) looking to join a community around these issues. We also encourage you to search for local groups in your own school communities, like the Detroit Community Technology Project (detroitcommunitytech.org/) that work directly with communities to ensure just, equitable, and creative implementations of technologies.

Participatory Action for Justice 3: Participate and/or Organize a Community School and Mutual Aid

Community schools are schools which provide wrap-around social services for a community which they serve. The National Education Association (NEA) describes community schools as centers that foster curiosity and offer the resources needed for students and communities to be physically and socially well, beyond the traditional extracurriculars, and including education, health, and career development for families.[11] Community schools offer a powerful place to implement AI interrogation and training for more just implementation, both with students and with the community. Although most teachers don't work in community schools, this is still a helpful model to look to for possible professional actions for your own school community.

Similarly, mutual aid models prioritize action-based community sharing, from the community and for the community. In this collaborative practice, small, community-based organizations offer ways to share resources. Knowledge of AI technologies could be part of a shared resource of mutual aid, including knowledge of how algorithms work, knowledge of how to code, how to prompt generative AI, and how to gather data about a community using a citizen scientist model. Participating in or organizing a technology mutual aid community organization can build civic connection and share knowledge about generative AI.

CONCLUSION

We hope that you have connected with some or all of the personal, pedagogical, professional, and participatory actions we have shared. Your dedication to ensuring that students have the opportunity to engage with AI technologies in safe ways that truly bring joyful experiences can be enacted through actions in each of these four areas. These examples are just starting points to what can be a long history of actions that not only impact your students but future generations. If you decide to take action, we would love to hear about how it went and what you plan to do moving forward. Onward!

REFLECTION QUESTIONS

After reading this chapter, reflect on the following questions related to personal, pedagogical, professional, and participatory actions.

1. What personal actions will I take to make change toward a more just use of AI?

2. What pedagogical actions will I take to make change toward a more just use of AI?
3. What professional actions will I take to make change toward a more just use of AI?
4. What participatory actions will I take to make change toward a more just use of AI?

CONCLUSION

Moving Forward: The Future of JustAI

> Urging all of us to open our minds and hearts so that we can know beyond the boundaries of what is acceptable, so that we can think and rethink, so that we can create new visions, I celebrate teaching that enables transgressions—a movement against and beyond boundaries. It is that movement which makes education the practice of freedom.
>
> —bell hooks, *Teaching to Transgress*

IN OUR BOOK WE TRAVELED the recent history of AI and educational technologies, underscoring the bias and injustice baked into their design and deployment. From the incomplete and majoritarian datasets which feed AI to the outputs which refuse to see darker skin, to the personalized learning "solutions" which elevate efficiency over care, intellect over affect, and knowledge over nurturing while divorcing the student from the system in which they learn, we offer examples of how AI technology has not succeeded in moving us toward a more just world. We include these histories not to deter nor discourage, but rather, because naming injustice is the first step in building more just technologies and education systems.

Next, we offered two paths forward for the future of education. One was more of the same as already paved by tech entrepreneurs like Thomas Edison, Sal Khan, Bill Gates, and Mark Zuckerberg. The other path offered a road less traveled, inspired by justice-oriented educators including

Carter G. Woodson, bell hooks, Gloria Ladson-Billings, Bettina Love, and Django Paris. These educators have worked toward the abolition of oppressive systems, embraced joy in resistance, and imagined new and more just futures.

We leaned into the mind-sets of criticality and technoskepticism to develop skills, knowledge, and dispositions oriented toward justice, exploring how mind-sets impact thoughts, feelings, beliefs and behaviors surrounding AI. We argued that teachers can play a role in changing the narratives of inevitability around technology, despite the prevalence, power, and influence of educational technology companies. We can make dispositional shifts toward AI in the classrooms based on technoskepticism, discriminatory design, and design justice.

To inspire just AI actions for change we turned to bell hooks' notion of *homeplace* as a site of resistance, nurturing, and critical consciousness, and considered it within schools. Teachers aiming to create homeplace in their classrooms must create antiracist, asset-based, nurturing spaces within the confines of the institution of school. We drew on the radical placemaking of homeplace to offer specific examples of how students and teachers might craft homeplace along and inside the geography of AI.

Springing from the homeplace as the site which nurtures actions, we turned to fugitive and abolitionist actions which can foster the good trouble of John Lewis and other activists who fight for freedom. Fugitive acts occur in the quiet resistance against unjust schools and technologies, and abolitionist pedagogies demand freedom dreaming, joy, and imagining new and more just ways for schools and technologies to exist. We reviewed existing movements for justice, including community organizations, opportunities to model and apply work from the Algorithmic Justice League in schools, and civic action projects students can take with and against AI.

Finally, we closed the book with specific actions that educators can take in different domains where they hold power: their personal lives, their professional lives, their pedagogical choices, and their participation in collective actions toward justice.

If we could sum up the lessons we hope readers draw from the book, it would be to teach using AI for justice and joy:

1. Name and acknowledge existing injustice in AI and schools.
2. Develop and lean into mind-sets of critical consciousness and technoskepticism.
3. Apply culturally sustaining, fugitive, and abolitionist pedagogies to teach judiciously with and about AI.
4. Take action in personal, pedagogical, professional, and participatory domains.

Because they are numbered, it may be tempting to read this as "four steps to just AI integration." However, we numbered them to indicate that while it helps to work through the actions consecutively, this is not a checklist and no action is ever marked as complete. Each area requires continued growth, learning, and reflection. Even with commitments to this work, we recognize there are significant challenges to implementation.

CHALLENGES ON THE HORIZON

First, it is unusual for education to not immediately accept the narrative of technology companies when integrating technology into schools. There is an over one-hundred-year history of schools cycling through hype, hope, and disappointment of wishing that the next technological innovation around the corner will be the "silver bullet" that solves education. It is the same with the rush to implement genAI in schools or risk the nebulous threat of "falling behind." However, what our book demonstrates is that it is unlikely that even the powerful technology of generative AI will fundamentally change education. What is much more likely is that genAI will fundamentally change *society*, and our job is to prepare students for a world where the promises and perils of genAI exist in their daily and collective lives. It is also our job to help students understand that they can imagine futures different from the ones told by technologies companies, and integration of AI with mind-sets of criticality and technoskepticism can help dream those futures.

Second, this book enumerates the ways that encoded bias within genAI and the embedded inequities of schooling in the US exist. It requires naming that injustice exists in all its forms, including racism, patriarchy, ableism, queerphobia, and so on, in order to act toward more just ends. We also recognize that it is illegal in some states in the US to teach about diversity, equity, and inclusion, and that the federal government is threatening to withhold funds from schools which teach toward equity. This can create a substantial challenge to implementing just AI in classrooms. We acknowledge this challenge and turn to educators who have modeled how to teach in oppressive and unjust spaces.

TOOLS OF THE BOOK TO HELP MEET CHALLENGES

In spite of the egregious harms of AI that we have acknowledged and warned against as we reviewed the historical and present impacts of AI, there are sound tools cultivated and articulated in this book that can support you in meeting the challenge that lies ahead. These tools are built on the foundation of equity-mindedness and critical consciousness, to lead us not to "Revolutionized" Education but toward the transformational transcendence of The Revolution.

As educators, the tools that are often most useful are the pedagogies that guide teaching and learning. Consequently, we have interwoven three equity-centered and antiracist pedagogical frameworks (culturally sustaining, fugitive, and abolitionist pedagogies) as tools to use when navigating AI technologies, with a main aim of providing joyful learning experiences for all students, while also aligning with the Hippocratic oath, which states "first, do no harm." It is not enough to just not do harm, although it is extremely important. Instead, you must recognize that that your action is power and use the tools we have to intentionally design learning experiences. When students engage with AI, which they

undoubtedly will, you must work to ensure that such engag
only not harmful to their physiological, psychological, or phys
but elevates the ebullience and excitement of learning.

Through the use of culturally responsive, relevant, and sustainin agogies, you have the tools required to create a homeplace in your cl rooms for students, guided by the wisdom of bell hooks. In your wor creating equitable and inclusive approaches to AI use across the curricula is possible, starting with a critical engagement with the outputs of one the most used AI chatbots, ChatGPT, and considering alternatives that may have more responsible framing in the code. For example, we shared Claude not as an exemplar, but to highlight its constitutional AI inclusions, with contrasting outputs to ChatGPT. You can lean into counterstorytelling to amplify student voice when using AI technologies or intentionally use specific platforms such as StoryAI, which was designed for culturally relevant learning experiences. You also are aware of tools and practices to lean into for ethical image generation, as well as the potential of walled gardens to keep out unvetted and harmful content. Your tools can support you in elevating the linguistic capital of multilingual students, ensuring that their home language is valued and honored within the homeplace you have cultivated.

These pedagogical tools will embolden you to make good trouble that is necessary to ensure that students have opportunities to engage with AI, in ways that do not harm them. You can pull from the tools of fugitive and abolitionist pedagogies, aligning your practices to those of algorithmic and AI justice. Moreover, you can take civic action and employ harm reduction pedagogical practices, nurturing digital futures that are built on equity.

LOOKING FORWARD

We acknowledge that AI has inherent flaws; however, we remain hopeful that through good struggle and the powerful pedagogy presented in the book, educators can democratize AI technologies by teaching students methods for judiciously and joyfully engaging with it. In centering good struggle in using JustAI, we suggest that when the pedagogies we shared in this book are anchored in the wisdom of marginalized educators, we can better navigate the incessant technological shifts the future will hold.

We would like to thank you for thoughtfully engaging with this book. As fellow educators, we realize this work is not easy. But, we also know that when we are empowered and prepared with resources, there is hope for a future that can be filled with joyous learning with and about AI.

NOTES

FOREWORD

1. Donna Haraway, "A Cyborg Manifesto: Science, Technology, and Socialist-Feminism in the Late Twentieth Century," in *Simians, Cyborgs and Women: The Reinvention of Nature* (Routledge, 1991).
2. Jamie Myers, "The Value-Laden Assumptions of Our Interpretive Practices," *Reading Research Quarterly* 30, no. 3 (1995): 582–87.

INTRODUCTION

1. Andrea Volpe, "The Cartes de Visite Craze," *New York Times*, August 6, 2013, https://archive.nytimes.com/opinionator.blogs.nytimes.com/2013/08/06/the-cartes-de-visite-craze.
2. Lorna Roth, "Looking at Shirley, the Ultimate Norm: Colour Balance, Image Technologies, and Cognitive Equity," *Canadian Journal of Communication* (2009), https://doi:10.22230/cjc.2009v34n1a2196.
3. Florian Koenigsberger, "Image Equity: Making Image Tools More Fair for Everyone," *The Keyword* (official Google blog), October 19, 2021, https://blog.google/products/pixel/image-equity-real-tone-pixel-6-photos/.
4. Jack Nicas, "Atlanta Asks Google Whether It Targeted Black Homeless People," *New York Times*, October 4, 2019, https://www.nytimes.com/2019/10/04/technology/google-facial-recognition-atlanta-homeless.html.
5. Jamilia J. Blake, Bettie Ray Butler, Chance W. Lewis, and Alicia Darensbourg, "Unmasking the Inequitable Discipline Experiences of Urban Black Girls: Implications for Urban Educational Stakeholders," *The Urban Review* 43 (2011): 90–106.
6. Wayne Au, *Unequal by Design: High-Stakes Testing and the Standardization of Inequality* (Routledge, 2022).
7. Richard Rothstein, "The Myth of De Facto Segregation," *Phi Delta Kappan* 100, no. 5 (2019): 35–38.

8. Ann Piccard, "Death by Boarding School: 'The Last Acceptable Racism' and the United States' Genocide of Native Americans," *Gonzaga Law Review* 49 (2013): 137.
9. Ruja Benjamin, "Assessing Risk, Automating Racism," *Science* 366, no. 6464 (2019): 421–22; Safiya Noble, *Algorithms of Oppression* (New York University Press, 2018); Sasha Costanza-Chock, *Design Justice: Community-Led Practices to Build the Worlds We Need* (The MIT Press, 2020).
10. Django Paris, "Culturally Sustaining Pedagogy: A Needed Change in Stance, Terminology, and Practice," *Educational Researcher* 41, no. 3 (2012), https://doi.org/10.3102/0013189X12441244.
11. Jarvis Givens, *Fugitive Pedagogy: Carter G. Woodson and the Art of Black Teaching* (Harvard University Press, 2023).
12. Bettina Love, *We Want to Do More Than Survive: Abolitionist Teaching and the Pursuit of Educational Freedom* (Beacon Press, 2019).
13. Emily M. Bender, Timnit Gebru, Angelina McMillan-Major, and Shmargaret Shmitchell, "On the Dangers of Stochastic Parrots: Can Language Models Be Too Big?" in *Proceedings of the 2021 ACM Conference on Fairness, Accountability, and Transparency* (Association for Computing Machinery, 2021), 610–623.
14. Ruha Benjamin, *Race After Technology: Abolitionist Tools for the New Jim Code* (Polity Press, 2019); Safiya Umoja Noble, "Algorithms of Oppression: How Search Engines Reinforce Racism," in *Algorithms of Oppression* (New York University Press, 2018).
15. Joy Buolamwini and Timnit Gebru, "Gender Shades: Intersectional Accuracy Disparities in Commercial Gender Classification," in *Conference on Fairness, Accountability and Transparency* (PMLR [Proceedings of Machine Learning Research], 2018).
16. T. J. Benedict, "The Computer Got it Wrong: Facial Recognition Technology and Establishing Probable Cause to Arrest," *Washington and Lee Law Review* 79 (2022): 849.
17. Robert Bartlett, Adair Morse, Richard Stanton, and Nancy Wallace, "Consumer-Lending Discrimination in the FinTech Era," *Journal of Financial Economics* 143, no. 1 (2022): 30–56.
18. Benjamin, "Assessing Risk, Automating Racism."
19. Jamie Manolev, Anna Sullivan, and Roger Slee, "The Datafication of Discipline: ClassDojo, Surveillance and a Performative Classroom Culture," in *The Datafication of Education* (Routledge, 2020).
20. Juan Del Toro and Ming-Te Wang, "The Roles of Suspensions for Minor Infractions and School Climate in Predicting Academic Performance Among Adolescents," *American Psychologist* 77, no. 2 (2022): 173.
21. International Society for Technology in Education (ISTE), "Artificial Intelligence in Education," website of ISTE, 2024, https://iste.org/ai.

22. Marie Heath, Sumreen Asim, Natalie Milman, and Jessa Henderson, "Confronting Tools of the Oppressor: Framing Just Technology Integration in Educational Technology and Teacher Education," *Contemporary Issues in Technology and Teacher Education* 22, no. 4 (2022): 754–77.
23. Natasha Singer and Daisuke Wakabyashi, "New Mexico Sues Google Over Children's Privacy Violations," *New York Times*, February 20, 2020, https://www.nytimes.com/2020/02/20/technology/new-mexico-google-lawsuit.html.
24. Benjamin Gleason and Marie K. Heath, "Injustice Embedded in Google Classroom and Google Meet: A Techno-Ethical Audit of Remote Educational Technologies," *Italian Journal of Educational Technology* 29, no. 2 (2021): 26–41.
25. Lynn Cuban, "Teachers and Machines: The Classroom Use of Technology Since 1920," *Teachers College Press* 2 (1986): 517–28.
26. Abeba Birhane, "Algorithmic Injustice: a Relational Ethics Approach," *Patterns* 2, no. 2 (2021).
27. Benjamin, *Race After Technology*.
28. Jacob Pleasants, Daniel G. Krutka, and T. Philip Nichols, "What Relationships Do We Want with Technology? Toward Technoskepticism in Schools," *Harvard Educational Review* 93, no. 4 (2023): 486–515.
29. Cathy O'Neil, *Weapons of Math Destruction: How Big Data Increases Inequality and Threatens Democracy* (Crown, 2017).
30. Reprint from bell hooks, "The Homeplace (A Site of Resistance)," in *Yearning: Race, Gender, and Cultural Politics* (South End Press, 1990).
31. Givens, *Fugitive Pedagogy*.
32. Love, *Pursuit of Educational Freedom*.
33. Patricia Hill Collins, *Black Feminist Thought* (Routledge, 2002), 223.

CHAPTER 1

1. Craig S. Smith, "A.I. Is Here, There, Everywhere," *New York Times*, February 23, 2021, https://www.nytimes.com/2021/02/23/technology/ai-innovation-privacy-seniors-education.html.
2. Ruha Benjamin, "Is Technology Our Savior—or Slayer?," TED Talk, October 2023, 11 min., 52 sec., https://www.ted.com/talks/ruha_benjamin_is_technology_our_savior_or_our_slayer.
3. Selin Akgun and Christine Greenhow, "Artificial Intelligence in Education: Addressing Ethical Challenges in K-12 Settings," *AI and Ethics* 2 (2022): 431–40.
4. The authors input the words "harms of AI" into the Google search engine.
5. Caleb Colón-Rodríguez, "Shedding Light on Healthcare Algorithmic and Artificial Intelligence Bias," *OMH News* (on the website of the US Department of Health and Human Services Office of Minority Health), July 12, 2023, https://minorityhealth.hhs.gov/news/shedding-light-healthcare-algorithmic-and-artificial-intelligence-bias.

6. Khadija Alhumaid, "Four Ways Technology Has Negatively Changed Education," *Journal of Educational and Social Research* 9, no. 4 (October 2019): 10–20, https://doi.org/10.2478/jesr-2019-0049.
7. Hugues Sampasa-Kanyinga, Hayley A. Hamilton, Gary S. Goldfield, and Chaput Jean-Phillippe, "Problem Technology Use, Academic Performance, and School Connectedness Among Adolescents," *International Journal of Environmental Research and Public Health* 19, no. 4 (February 2022): 2337, https://doi: 10.3390/ijerph19042337.
8. Ben Shneiderman, *Human-Centered AI* (Oxford University Press, 2022).
9. National Library of Medicine (NLM), "Algorithm," website of the NLM, https://www.nnlm.gov/guides/data-glossary/algorithm.
10. Stephanie Smith Budhai and Kristine Lewis Grant, *Culturally Responsive Teaching Online and In-Person: An Action Planner for Dynamic Equitable Learning Environments* (Corwin, 2022).
11. Cambridge English Dictionary, "Data," website of the Cambridge English Dictionary, https://dictionary.cambridge.org/us/dictionary/english/data#google_vignette.
12. IBM (International Business Machines Corporation), "What is a Neural Network?," website of IBM, https://www.ibm.com/topics/neural-networks.
13. National Center for Science and Engineering Statistics (NCSES) Directorate for Social, Behavioral and Economic Sciences, *Diversity and STEM: Women, Minorities, and Persons with Disabilities, 2023* (National Science Foundation, 2023), https://ncses.nsf.gov/pubs/nsf23315/.
14. Larry Hardesty, "Explained: Neural Networks," *MIT News*, April 14, 2017, paragraph 7, https://news.mit.edu/2017/explained-neural-networks-deep-learning-0414.
15. Abeba Birhane, "Algorithmic Injustice: A Relational Ethics Approach," *Patterns* 2, no. 2 (2021).
16. Ben Tarnoff, "Weizenbaum's Nightmares: How the Inventor of the First Chatbot Turned Against AI," *The Guardian*, July 25, 2023.
17. Robert Bartlett, Adair Morse, Richard Stanton, and Nancy Wallace, "Consumer-Lending Discrimination in the FinTech Era," *Journal of Financial Economics* 143, no, 1 (2022): 30–56.
18. Mark Weber, Mikhail Yurochkin, Sherif Botros, and Vanio Markov, "Black Loans Matter: Distributionally Robust Fairness for Fighting Subgroup Discrimination," arXiv preprint (2020), https://arxiv.org/abs/2012.01193.
19. "Apple's 'Sexist' Credit Card Investigated by US Regulator," *BBC*, November 11, 2019, https://www.bbc.com/news/business-50365609.
20. Office of Public Affairs, "Justice Department and Consumer Financial Protection Bureau Sue Texas-Based Developer and Lender Colony Ridge for Bait-and-Switch Land Sales and Predatory Financing," website of the US Department of

43. Jamie Manolev, Anna Sullivan, and Roger Slee, "The Datafication of Discipline: ClassDojo, Surveillance and a Performative Classroom Culture," in *The Datafication of Education* (Routledge, 2020).
44. Ben Williamson, Alex Molnar, and Faith Boninger, "Time for a Pause: Without Effective Public Oversight, AI in Schools Will Do More Harm Than Good," website of the National Education Policy Center, 2024, https://nepc.colorado.edu/publication/ai.
45. Melissa Warr, "The Battle of LLMs and ELLs," *Capricious Connections* (blog), April 3, 2024, https://melissa-warr.com/llms-and-ells/.
46. Paulo Freire, *Pedagogy of the Oppressed* (Seabury Press, 1974).
47. Geling Xu, Aerin Benavides, Angela Calabrese Barton, Edna Tan, Selena Bliesener, Gina DiFrancesco, and Scott Calabrese Barton, "Critical Consciousness in Engineering for Sustainable Communities," website of the National Science Teaching Association, 2022, https://www.nsta.org/connected-science-learning/connected-science-learning-january-february-2022/critical-consciousness.
48. Henry Giroux, "Teachers as Transformatory Intellectuals," Symposium on Understanding Quality Education: Conference on Re-Envisioning Quality in Education, https://itacec.org/afed/document/henry_giroux_2_ok.pdf.
49. Giroux, "Teachers as Transformatory Intellectuals."
50. MIT (Massachusetts Institute of Technology), letter regarding withdrawal of the 80 Million Tiny Images dataset, June 29, 2020, https://groups.csail.mit.edu/vision/TinyImages/.
51. Katherine Norris, Lisa Lucas, and Catherine Prudhoe, "Examining Critical Literacy in the Early Childhood Classroom," *Promising Practices* (Winter 2012): 59, https://files.eric.ed.gov/fulltext/EJ1001528.pdf.
52. Bill Schmarzo, *AI & Data Literacy: Empowering Citizens of Data Science* (Packt Publishing, 2023).
53. Allen Luke, "Critical Approaches to Literacy," in *Encyclopedia of Language and Education Vol 2.: Literacy*, ed. Viv Edwards and David Corson (Springer, 1997), https://link.springer.com/chapter/10.1007/978-94-011-4540-4_16.
54. Gloria Ladson-Billings and William F. Tate, "Toward a Critical Theory of Education," *Teachers College Record* 97, no. 2 (September 1995): 47–68.
55. Tiera Tanksley, "'We're Changing the System with This One': Black Students Using Critical Race Algorithmic Literacies to Subvert and Survive AI-Mediated Racism in Schools," *English Teaching: Practice and Critique* 23, no. 2 (2024): 3, https://doi:10.1108/ETPC-08-2023-0102.
56. Tanksley, "We're Changing the System."
57. Tanksley, "We're Changing the System."
58. Luci Pangrazio and Neil Selwyn, "'Personal Data Literacies': A Critical Literacies Approach to Enhancing Understandings of Personal Digital," *New Media & Society* 21, no. 2 (2018).

59. Tim Stobierski, "Data Literacy: An Introduction for Business," Harvard Business School Online, https://online.hbs.edu/blog/post/data-literacy.
60. Pangrazio and Selwyn, "Personal Data Literacies."
61. Pangrazio and Selwyn, "Personal Data Literacies."
62. Pangrazio and Selwyn, "Personal Data Literacies," 429.
63. Jiahong Su and Yuchun Zhong, "Artificial Intelligence (AI) in Early Childhood Education: Curriculum Design and Future Directions," *Computers and Education: Artificial Intelligence* (2022), https://doi.org/10.1016/j.caeai.2022.100072.
64. Seonghum Kim, "Why and What to Teach: AI Curriculum for Elementary School," *Proceedings of the 35th AAAI Conference on Artificial Intelligence* (Association for the Advancement of Artificial Intelligence [AAAI], 2021), https://ojs.aaai.org/index.php/AAAI/article/view/17833.
65. Alex Hanna, Emily Denton, Andrew Smart, and Jamila Smith-Lord, "Towards a Critical Race Methodology," in *FAT* '20: Proceedings of the 2020 Conference on Fairness, Accountability, and Transparency* (Association for Computing Machinery, 2020), https://doi.org/10.1145/3351095.3372826.

CHAPTER 2

1. Frederick James Smith, "The Evolution of the Motion Picture," *The New York Dramatic Mirror,* July 9, 1913, http://www.laviemoderne.net/images/forum_pics/2017/20171116%20New%20York%20NY%20Dramatic%20Mirror%201913%20Mar-Apr%201914%20Grayscale%20-%200690.pdf.
2. Virginia Woodson Frame Church, "Antiquated," in *Teachers Are People, Being the Lyrics of Agatha Brown, Sometime Teacher in the Hilldale High School* (Authors Publishing Corporation, 1925).
3. Larry Cuban, *Teachers and Machines: The Classroom Use of Technology Since 1920* (Teachers College Press, 1986).
4. Audrey Watters, *Teaching Machines: The History of Personalized Learning* (The MIT Press, 2023).
5. B. F. Skinner, "Teaching Machines: From The Experimental Study of Learning Come Devices Which Arrange Optimal Conditions for Self-Instruction," *Science* 128, no. 3330 (1958): 969–77.
6. Watters, *Teaching Machines.*
7. Sidney L. Pressey, "A Third and Fourth Contribution Toward the Coming 'Industrial Revolution' in Education," *School & Society* (1932).
8. Daniel Seligman, "The Low Productivity of the 'Education Industry,'" *Fortune,* 135–38, 295–96.
9. Joseph N. Bell, "Will Robots Teach Your Children?," *Popular Mechanics* 116, no. 4 (October, 1961), 152–57, 246.
10. Alfred Bork, "Millikan Lecture," lecture given at the American Association of Physics Teachers, London, Ontario, June 1978; appeared in the *American Journal of Physics* 47, no. 1 (January 1979).

11. Dreambox, official website of Dreambox, https://www.dreambox.com/; iReady, official website of iReady, https://ireadycentral.com/familycenter/what-is-i-ready/.
12. Eduardo Bonilla-Silva, *Racism Without Racists: Color-Blind Racism and the Persistence of Racial Inequality in the United States* (Rowman & Littlefield Publishers, 2006).
13. Lois Weis and Michelle Fine, "Critical Bifocality and Circuits of Privilege: Expanding Critical Ethnographic Theory and Design," *Harvard Educational Review* 82, no. 2 (2012): 173–201, 175–76, emphasis ours.
14. Carlo Perrotta. Kalervo N. Gulson, Ben Williamson, and Kevin Witzenberger, "Automation, APIs and the Distributed Labour of Platform Pedagogies in Google Classroom," *Critical Studies in Education* 62, no. 1 (2021): 97–113.
15. Google, home page, Google for Education website, https://edu.google.com/.
16. Andrea Petersen, "Google Is Tracking Students as It Sells More Products to Schools, Privacy Advocates Warn," *The Washington Post,* December 28, 2015, https://www.washingtonpost.com/news/the-switch/wp/2015/12/28/google-is-tracking-students-as-it-sells-more-products-to-schools-privacy-advocates-warn/.
17. Olina Banerji, "Schools Are Using Voice Technology to Teach Reading. Is It Helping?" EdSurge, March 7, 2023, https://www.edsurge.com/news/2023-03-07-schools-are-using-voice-technology-to-teach-reading-is-it-helping.
18. Riddhi Divanji, Samantha Bindman, Allie Tung, Katherine Chen, Lisa Castaneda, and Mike Scanlon, "A One Stop Shop? Perspectives on the Value of Adaptive Learning Technologies in K-12 Education," *Computers and Education Open* 5, no. 100157 (2023): 1–14.
19. Chein-Chang Lin, Anna Huang, and Owen Lu, "Artificial Intelligence in Intelligent Tutoring Systems Toward Sustainable Education: A Systematic Review," *Smart Learning Environments* 10, no. 41 (2023): 1–22.
20. Huanhuan Wang, Ahmed Tlili, Ronghuai Huang, Zhenyu Cai, Min Li, Zui Cheng, Dong Yang, Mengti Li, Xixian Zhu, and Cheng Fei, "Examining the Applications of Intelligent Tutoring Systems in Real Educational Contexts: A Systematic Literature Review from the Social Experiment Perspective," *Education and Information Technologies* 28 (2023): 9113–48.
21. Stacey Lutz and Wiliam Huitt, "Connecting Cognitive Development and Constructivism: Implications from Theory for Instruction and Assessment," *Constructivism in the Human Sciences* 9, no. 1 (2004): 1–17, https://www.edpsycinteractive.org/papers/cogdev.pdf.
22. Wilson J. Moses, "W.E.B. Du Bois's 'The Conservation of Races' and Its Context: Idealism, Conservatism and Hero Worship," *The Massachusetts Review* 34, no. 2 (1993): 275–94, http://www.jstor.org/stable/25090431.
23. Divanji et al., "One Stop Shop?"
24. Johanna Velander, Mohammed Ahmed Taiye, Nuno Otero, Marcelo Milrad Otero, "Artificial Intelligence in K-12 Education: Eliciting and Reflecting on

Swedish Teachers' Understanding of AI and Its Implications for Teaching & Learning," *Education and Information Technologies* 29 (2024): 4085–105.

25. Arianna Protheo, "See Which Types of Teachers Are the Early Adopters of AI," *Education Week*, April 17, 2024, https://www.edweek.org/technology/see-which-types-of-teachers-are-the-early-adopters-of-ai/2024/04.
26. Protheo, "Which Types of Teachers."
27. Ismail Celik, "Towards Intelligent-TPACK: An Empirical Study on Teachers' Professional Knowledge to Ethically Integrate Artificial Intelligence (AI)-Based Tools into Education," *Computers in Human Behavior* 138, no. 107468 (2023): 1–2.
28. Yavar Bathaee, "The Artificial Intelligence Black Box and the Failure of Intent and Causation," *Harvard Journal of Law & Technology* 31, No 2 (2018): 890–934, 905, https://jolt.law.harvard.edu/assets/articlePDFs/v31/The-Artificial-Intelligence-Black-Box-and-the-Failure-of-Intent-and-Causation-Yavar-Bathaee.pdf.
29. Rodrigo Smiderle, Sandro Jose Rigo, Leonardo Marques, Jorge Pecanha de Miranda Coelho, and Patricia Jaques, "The Impact of Gamification on Students' Learning, Engagement and Behavior Based on Their Personality Traits," *Smart Learning Environments* 7, no. 3 (2020): 1–11.
30. Elias Ratinho and Catia Martins, "The Role of Gamified Learning Strategies in Student's Motivation in High School and Higher Education: A Systematic Review," *Heliyon* 9, no. 8 (2023): 1–16.
31. Minecraft Education, "Build with the Agent," website of Minecraft, https://education.minecraft.net/en-us/lessons/build-with-the-agent.
32. Chen Yuki, Jonaya Kemper, Erik Harpstead, Ross Higashi, and Judith Uchidiuno, "Designing Black Children in Video Games," *Interactions* (September–October 2023), https://dl.acm.org/doi/pdf/10.1145/3610968.
33. Yuki et al., "Designing Black Children."
34. Victoria Turk, "The Rise of AI: How AI Reduces the World to Stereotypes," *Rest of the World*, October 10, 2023, https://restofworld.org/2023/ai-image-stereotypes/.
35. Leonardo Nicoletti and Dina Bass, "Humans are biased: Generative AI is Even Worse," June 9, 2023, *Bloomberg*, https://www.bloomberg.com/graphics/2023-generative-ai-bias/.
36. Natalie Fear, "Fortnite Has a Problem with Racist AI Art," February 1, 2024, Creative Bloq, https://www.creativebloq.com/news/fortnite-racist-ai-images.
37. David Melhart, Julian Togelius, Benedikte Mikkelsen, Christoffer Holmgard, and Georgios Yannakakis, "The Ethics of AI in Games," *IEEE: Institute of Electrical and Electronics Engineers* 15, no. 1 (2024): 79–92.
38. Melhard et al., "AI in Games."
39. Yoones Sekhavat, Samad Roohi, Hesam Mohammadi, and Georgios Yannakakis, "Play With One's Feelings: A Study on Emotion Awareness for Player Experience," *IEEE Transactions on Games*, (2020): 1–10.

40. Alessandro Mascellino, "We Need to Address the Ethics of AI in Video," *Techopedia*, October 26, 2023, https://www.techopedia.com/ethics-of-ai-in-video-games; Stephen Molchan, "We Can Do More: COVID-19's Spotlight on the Lack of Financial Literacy," *Journal of Family and Consumer Sciences* 115, no. 1 (2023): 10–13.
41. Lasha Labadze, Maya Grigolia, and Lela Machaidze, "Role of AI Chatbots in Education: Systematic Literature Review," *International Journal of Educational Technology in Higher Education* 20, no. 56 (2023): 1–17.
42. Enkeleja Kasneci, Kathrin Seßler, Stefan Küchemann, Maria Bannert, Daryna Dementieva, Frank Fischer, et al., "ChatGPT For Good? On Opportunities and Challenges of Large Language Models for Education," *Learning and Individual Differences* 103, no. 102274 (2023): 1–9.
43. Nabeel Gillani, Rebecca Eynon, Catherine Chiabaut, and Kelsey Finkel, "Unpacking the 'Black Box' of AI in Education," *Educational Technology and Society* 26, no. 1 (2023): 99–111.
44. A.W. Ohlhesier, "AI Automated Discrimination: Here's How to Spot It," *Vox*, June 14, 2023, https://www.vox.com/technology/23738987/racism-ai-automated-bias-discrimination-algorithm.
45. Ohlhesier, "AI Automated Discrimination."
46. Marie Heath, Daniel Krutka, and Stephanie Smith Budhai, "Cultivating AI Criticality with Students Through Resistance, Refusal, and Reclamation," in *Policy Insights: AI and Digital Inequities* (Geneva Graduate Institute, NORRAG Global Education Centre, 2024).
47. Ohio Memory, "The Flame of Living Genius: The Ohio Air School of the Air," website of Ohio Memory, June 23, 2017, https://ohiomemory.ohiohistory.org/archives/3356.
48. William Bianchi, "Education by Radio: America's Schools of the Air," *Tech Trends* 52, no. 2 (2008): 36–45, https://wcftr.commarts.wisc.edu/wp-content/uploads/2015/02/Bianchi.pdf.
49. Bianchi, "Education by Radio."
50. Hope Kentnor, "Distance Education and the Evolution of Online Learning in the United States," *Curriculum and Teaching Dialogue* 17, no. 1–2 (2015): 21–34.
51. Smith, "Evolution of the Motion Picture."
52. Guilherme Giantini, "The Sophistry of the Neutral Tool, Weaponizing Artificial Intelligence and Big Data into Threats Towards Social Exclusion," *AI and Ethics* 3 (2023): 1049–61.
53. Morgan Stanley, "Generative AI is Set to Shake Up Education," website of Morgan Stanley, December 22, 2023, https://www.morganstanley.com/ideas/generative-ai-education-outlook.
54. Cambridge English Dictionary, "Tech Bro," website of the Cambridge English Dictionary, https://dictionary.cambridge.org/us/dictionary/english/tech-bro.

55. Greta Byrum and Ruha Benjamin, "Disrupting the Gospel of Tech Solutionism to Build Tech Justice," *Stanford Social Innovation Review*, 2022. https://doi.org/10.48558/9SEV-4D26.
56. Ruha Benjamin, "Is Technology Our Savior—or Slayer?," TED Talk, October 2023, 11 min., 52 sec., https://www.ted.com/talks/ruha_benjamin_is_technology_our_savior_or_our_slayer.
57. Marie K. Heath and Dan G. Krutka, "Is Technology Our Savior—or Our Slayer?: Ruha Benjamin's New TED Talk," *Civics of Technology* (blog), November 13, 2023.

CHAPTER 3

1. American Psychological Association, "Mindset," *APA Dictionary of Psychology*, https://dictionary.apa.org/mindset.
2. Sonja Laine and Kirsi Tirri, "Literature Review on Teachers' Mindsets, Growth-Oriented Practices, and Why They Matter," *Frontiers in Education* 8 (2023), https://www.frontiersin.org/journals/education/articles/10.3389/feduc.2023.1275126/full.
3. American Psychological Association, "Mindset."
4. American Psychological Association, "Thought," *APA Dictionary of Psychology*, https://dictionary.apa.org/mindset.
5. American Psychological Association, "Belief," *APA Dictionary of Psychology*, https://dictionary.apa.org/mindset.
6. American Psychological Association, "Attitude," *APA Dictionary of Psychology*, https://dictionary.apa.org/attitude.
7. American Psychological Association, "Behavior," *APA Dictionary of Psychology*, https://dictionary.apa.org/behavior.
8. Daniel Muijs and David Reynolds, "Teachers' Beliefs and Behaviors: What Really Matters?," *Journal of Classroom Interaction* 37, no. 2 (2002), reprinted 2015, https://files.eric.ed.gov/fulltext/EJ1100408.pdf.
9. Debra Crouch and Brian Camborne, "Why a Teacher's Beliefs Matter: Using A Theory of Learning to Explore Instructional Decisions," *The Journal of Reading Recovery* 22, no.1 (2022), https://www.teachingdecisions.com/wp-content/uploads/2022/11/JRR_22-1_fall_2022_crouch_cambourne.pdf.
10. Salomé Cojean, Laurent Brun, Franck Amadieu, and Philippe Dessus, "Teachers' Attitudes Towards AI: What is the Difference with Non-AI Technologies?," *Proceedings of the Annual Meeting of the Cognitive Science Society* 45 (2023): 2070, https://escholarship.org/uc/item/0r55s1jb.
11. Amber McKinney, "Educator Mindsets Affect Student Performance," website of the Northwest Evaluation Association, July 13, 2023, https://www.nwea.org/blog/2023/educator-mindsets-affect-student-performance/.
12. Felicitas Macgilchrist, "What is 'Critical' in Critical Studies of Edtech? Three Responses," *Learning, Media, and Technology* 46, no. 3 (2021): 244, https://www

.tandfonline.com/doi/epdf/10.1080/17439884.2021.1958843?needAccess =true.

13. Daniel G. Krutka and James Damico, "Should We Ask Students to Tweet?: Perceptions, Patterns, and Problems of Assigned Social Media Participation," *Contemporary Issues in Technology and Teacher Education* 84, no 2 (2020).
14. Joohnyeong Park, Tang Wee Teo, Arnold Teo, Jina Chang, Jun Son Huang, and Sengmeng Koo, "Integrating Artificial Intelligence into Science Lessons: Teachers' Experiences and Views," *International Journal of STEM Education* 10, no. 61 (2023).
15. Joshua A. Ellis, "Technology in Teacher Education: Science, Society, and Students," website of the American Association for the Advancement of Science, https://aaas-arise.org/2023/03/21/technology-in-teacher-education-science -society-and-students/.
16. Alison Beard, "Can Big Tech Be Disrupted?," *Harvard Business Review* (January–February 2022), https://hbr.org/2022/01/can-big-tech-be-disrupted.
17. Jonathan A. Knee, "Review: Two Contrasting Views of Silicon Valley's Influence," *New York Times*, November 10, 2017, https://www.nytimes.com/2017/11/10 /business/review-two-contrasting-views-of-silicon-valleys-influence.html.
18. Ramishah Maruf, "Amazon's Cashier-less Technology Was Supposed to Revolutionize Grocery Shopping. It's Been a Flop," *CNN*, April 3, 2024, https://www .cnn.com/2024/04/03/business/amazons-self-checkout-technology-grocery -flop/index.html.
19. "Amazon Go," clip from season 47 of Saturday Night Live, posted March 12, 2022, by Saturday Night Live, YouTube, https://www.youtube.com/watch?v =zS9U3Gc832Y.
20. Allison Klein, "Most Tech Companies Profit Off Student Data, Even If They Say Otherwise, Report Finds," *Education Week*, July 18, 2023, https://www.edweek .org/technology/most-tech-companies-profit-off-student-data-even-if-they -say-otherwise-report-finds/2023/07.
21. Kali Thompson, "The Cruel Optimism of Educational Technology Teacher Ambassador Spaces," *Power and Education* 16.2 (2024): 150–165.
22. Miao Lu and Jack Linchuan Qiu, "Empowerment of Warfare? Dark Skin, AI Camera, and Transsion's Patent Narrative," *Information, Communication & Society* 6 (2022): 768–84, https://doi.org/10.1080/1369118X.2022.2056500.
23. Jennifer Chubb, Darren Reed, and Peter Cowling, "Expert Views about Missing AI Narratives: Is There an AI Story Crisis?," *Open Forum* 39 (2024): 1107–26, https://link.springer.com/article/10.1007/s00146-022-01548-2.
24. Daniel G. Krutka, Autumm Caines, Marie K. Heath, and K. B. Staudt Willet, "Black Mirror Pedagogy: Dystopian Stories for Technoskeptical Imaginations," *The Journal of Interactive Technology and Pedagogy* 11, no. 1 (2022), https://cuny .manifoldapp.org/read/black-mirror-pedagogy-dystopian-stories-for

-technoskeptical-imaginations-5df256c8-ca16-45e1-9d1a-e68593443990/section/962a7c17-50d0-4e7a-aafe-483d077ed4bb.

25. Jacob Pleasants, Daniel G. Krutka, and T. Philip Nichols, "What Relationships Do We Want with Technology? Toward Technoskepticism in Schools," *Harvard Educational Review* 93, no. 4 (2023): 486–515; Daniel G. Krutka, Marie K. Heath, and Lance E. Mason, "Technology Won't Save Us–A Call for Technoskepticism in Social Studies," *Contemporary Issues in Technology and Teacher Education* 20, no. 1 (2020): 108–20.
26. Mark Sellman and Adam Vaughan, "'Thirsty' ChatGPT Uses Four Times More Water Than Previously Thought, *The Times*, October 4, 2024, https://www.thetimes.com/uk/technology-uk/article/thirsty-chatgpt-uses-four-times-more-water-than-previously-thought-bc0pqswdr.
27. Ali M. McManus, Philip N. Ainslie, Daniel J. Green, Ryan G. Simair, Kurt Smith, and Nia Lewis, "Impact of Prolonged Sitting on Vascular Function in Young Girls," *Experimental Physiology* 100, no. 11 (2015): 1379–87.
28. For more detailed ways that educators have responded to these questions in professional development settings, we encourage readers to read through the Civics of Technology blog post "Collectively Asking Technoskeptical Questions About ChatGPT," at https://www.civicsoftechnology.org/blog/collectively-asking-technoskeptical-questions-about-chatgpt.
29. Ruha Benjamin, *Race After Technology: Abolitionist Tools for the New Jim Code* (John Wiley & Sons, 2019), 5–6.
30. D. G. Krutka, R. Z. Seitz, and A. M. Hadi, "How Do We Oppose Racist Zoombombs?: A Discriminatory Design Technology Audit," *Teaching, Technology, and Teacher Education During the COVID-19 Pandemic: Stories from the Field* (2020): 753–59.
31. Tom Simonate, "Algorithms Were Supposed to Fix the Bail System, They Haven't," February 19, 2020, *Wired*, https://www.wired.com/story/algorithms-supposed-fix-bail-system-they-havent/.

CHAPTER 4

1. Reprint from bell hooks, "The Homeplace (a Site of Resistance)," in *Yearning: Race, Gender, and Cultural Politics* (Routledge, 2014).
2. Berea College: Hutchins Library, "In Memoriam: bell hooks," website of the Hutchins Library, January 27, 2022, https://libraryguides.berea.edu/c.php?g=1217612.
3. Emily Pullen, "Where to Start with bell hooks," website of the New York Public Library, December 15, 2021, https://www.nypl.org/blog/2021/12/15/where-start-bell-hooks.
4. hooks, "Homeplace."
5. bell hooks, *Yearning: Race, Gender, and Cultural Politics*, 2nd ed. (Routledge, 2014).
6. hooks, "Homeplace," 384.

7. Lauren Leigh Kelly, "'I Love Us for Real': Exploring Homeplace as a Site of Healing and Resistance for Black Girls in Schools," *Equity & Excellence in Education* 53, no. 4 (2020): 449–64.
8. Katherine McKittrick, "Freedom is a Secret: The Future Usability of the Underground," in *Black Geographies and the Politics of Place*, ed. Katherine McKittrick and Clyde Woods (Between the Lines, 2007).
9. Common Sense Media, "The Dawn of the AI Era: Teens, Parents, and the Adoption of Generative AI at Home and School," September 18, 2024, 16. https://www.commonsensemedia.org/research/the-dawn-of-the-ai-era-teens-parents-and-the-adoption-of-generative-ai-at-home-and-school.
10. Gloria Ladson-Billings, "Towards a Theory of Culturally Relevant Teaching," *American Educational Research Journal* 32, no. 3 (1994): 465–91.
11. Geneva Gay, *Culturally Responsive Teaching, Theory, Practice, and Research* (Teachers College Press, 2000).
12. Django Paris, "Culturally Sustaining Pedagogy: A Needed Change in Stance, Terminology, and Practice," *Educational Researcher* 41, no. 3 (2012): 93–97.
13. Lauren Midgette, "ChatGPT in the Culturally Relevant Classroom," Center for Professional Education of Teachers, Teachers College, Columbia University, https://cpet.tc.columbia.edu/news-press/chatgpt-in-the-culturally-relevant-classroom.
14. Lani Guinier, "From Racial Liberalism to Racial Literacy: *Brown v. Board of Education* and the Interest-Divergence Dilemma," *Journal of American History* (June 2004).
15. Yolanda-Sealey-Ruiz, *Racial Literacy*, website of the National Council of Teachers of English (NCTE), 2021, p. 2, https://ncte.org/wp-content/uploads/2021/04/SquireOfficePolicyBrief_RacialLiteracy_April2021.pdf.
16. AI 4 Social Progress (AI4SP), "From Bias to Inclusion: Training Data and AI Ethics," website of AI4SP, September 27, 2024, https://ai4sp.org/from-bias-to-inclusion-training-data-and-ai-ethics/.
17. Jeff Raikes, "AI Can Be Racist: Let's Make Sure It Works for Everyone," *Forbes*, April 21, 2023, https://www.forbes.com/sites/jeffraikes/2023/04/21/ai-can-be-racist-lets-make-sure-it-works-for-everyone/.
18. Anthropic, "Claude's Constitution," website of Anthropic, May 9, 2023, https://www.anthropic.com/news/claudes-constitution.
19. Anthropic, "Claude's Constitution," states "The UN declaration of Human Rights, having been drafted by representatives with different legal and cultural backgrounds and ratified (at least in part) by all 193 member states of the UN, seemed one of the most representative sources of human values we could find."
20. Amelia Glaese, Nat McAleese, Maja Trebacz, John Aslanides, Vlad Firoiu, Timo Ewalds et al., "Improving Alignment of Dialogue Agents Via Targeted Human Judgements," Deep Mind, September 20, 2022, https://storage.googleapis.com/deepmind-media/DeepMind.com/Authors-Notes/sparrow/sparrow-final.pdf.
21. Anthropic, "Claude's Constitution."

22. Daniel Solórzano and Tara Yosso, "Critical Race Methodology: Counterstorytelling as an Analytic Framework for Educational Research," *Qualitative Inquiry* 8, no. 1 (2002): 23–44, 32.
23. Shani Murray, "AIStory: Leveraging Generative AI for Culturally Responsive Learning," website of the UCI (University of California, Irvine) Department of Informatics, May 23, 2023, https://www.informatics.uci.edu/aistory-leveraging-generative-ai-for-culturally-responsive-learning/.
24. Tara J. Yosso, "Whose Culture Has Capital? A Critical Race Theory Discussion of Community Cultural Wealth," *Race, Ethnicity and Education* 8, no. 1 (2005): 69–91.
25. Tan Huynh, "Using AI to Support Multilingual Students," *Edutopia*, November 21, 2023, https://www.edutopia.org/article/using-ai-support-multilingual-students/
26. Jeff Horowitz and Katherine Blunt, "Instagram Connects Vast Pedophile Network," *The Wall Street Journal*, June 7, 2023, https://www.wsj.com/articles/instagram-vast-pedophile-network-4ab7189.
27. Tess, official website of Tess, https://www.tess.design/.
28. Alyson Klien, "Welcome to the 'Walled Garden': Is This Education's Solution to AI's Pitfalls?," *Education Week*, July 25, 2023, https://www.edweek.org/technology/welcome-to-the-walled-garden-is-this-educations-solution-to-ais-pitfalls/2023/07.
29. Refik Anadol, "Unsupervised," mixed-media, displayed at the Museum of Modern Art (MoMa), New York, from November 19, 2022 to October 29, 2023, https://www.moma.org/calendar/exhibitions/5535.
30. Joan Kee and Michelle Kuo, "Deep Learning: AI, Art History, and the Museum," website of MoMa, June 15, 2023, https://www.moma.org/magazine/articles/839.
31. Katherine McKittrick, *Demonic Grounds: Black Women and the Cartographies of Struggle* (University of Minnesota Press, 2006).
32. Jill Barshay, "Researchers Combat AI Hallucinations in Math," *Hechinger Report*, August 26, 2024, https://hechingerreport.org/proof-points-combat-ai-hallucinations-math/.
33. Melaina Cecilia de la Cruz, "7 Latinos in AI to Watch," *Hispanic Executive*, July 16, 2024, https://hispanicexecutive.com/latinos-in-ai-to-watch/.
34. "The Global Cultural Lens of AI," interview with Laura N. Montoya, by Just Digital Future for the Harvard Business School, https://www.hbs.edu/race-gender-equity/projects/just-digital-future/Pages/video.aspx?item=laura-montoya.
35. Cruz, "7 Latinos."
36. Stanford University, "Fei-Fei Li," Stanford Profiles, https://profiles.stanford.edu/fei-fei-li.
37. The Ohio State University College of Engineering, "About Dean Ayanna Howard," website of the College of Engineering, https://engineering.osu.edu/about/office-dean/about-dean-ayanna-howard.

38. National Science Foundation (NSF), National Center for Science and Engineering Statistics (NCSES), "Diversity and STEM: Women, Minorities, and Persons with Disabilities," NCSES website, https://ncses.nsf.gov/pubs/nsf23315/report/the-stem-workforce#representation-in-the-stem-workforce (page removed).
39. Tomiko Oskotsky, Ruchika Bajaj, Jillian Burchard, Taylor Cavazos, Ina Chen, William T. Connell et al., "Nurturing Diversity and Inclusion in AI in Biomedicine Through a Virtual Summer Program for High School Students," *PLoS Computational Biology* 18, no. 1 (Jan 31 2022).
40. UCSF (University of California, San Francisco) AI4ALL, website of AI4ALL, https://ai4all.ucsf.edu/index.html.
41. Maria Mercone, "The Homeplace, the Margin and the Classroom: Mapping Radical Liberation," *USAbroad: Journal of American History and Politics* 6 (2023).
42. bell hooks, *Belonging: A Culture of Place* (Routledge, 2009).
43. Dimitri Kanaris, "Unlock The Power of AI in Your Classroom with Kahoot's New Question Generator!," Kahoot blog, June 6, 2023, https://kahoot.com/blog/2023/06/06/kahoot-ai/.

CHAPTER 5

1. Terrence L. Johnson, "Moral Faith and the Legacy of John Lewis's Political Vision of 'Good Trouble.'" *The Journal of Law and Religion* 37, no. 1 (2022): 37–45, https://doi:https://doi.org/10.1017/jlr.2021.74.
2. Erin Blakemore, "John Lewis' Arrest Records Are Finally Uncovered: "Good Trouble" Led to Real Consequences for the Civil Rights Agitator," *Smithsonian Magazine*, December 1, 2016.
3. Carla D. Hayden, "Remembering John Lewis: The Power of 'Good Trouble,'" *TIMELESS: Stories from the Library of Congress* (blog), July 19, 2020, https://blogs.loc.gov/loc/2020/07/remembering-john-lewis-the-power-of-good-trouble/.
4. Jarvis R. Givens, *Fugitive Pedagogy: Carter G. Woodson and the Art of Black Teaching* (Harvard University Press, 2021).
5. Bettina L. Love, *We Want to Do More Than Survive: Abolitionist Teaching and the Pursuit of Educational Freedom* (Beacon Press, 2019).
6. Scott Neuman, "The Culture Wars Are Pushing Some Teachers to Leave the Classroom," *NPR*, November 13, 2020, https://www.npr.org/2022/11/13/1131872280/teacher-shortage-culture-wars-critical-race-theory.
7. Giulia Heyward and Juma Sei, "College Board's Revised AP African American Studies Course Draws New Criticism," *NPR*, February 1, 2023, https://www.npr.org/2023/02/01/1153434464/college-boards-revised-ap-african-american-studies-course-draws-new-criticism.
8. Spencer Terry, "Florida School District Orders Removal of All Books with Gay Characters Before Slightly Backing Off," *AP News*, September 27, 2023, https://apnews.com/article/lgbtq-florida-dont-say-gay-books-bed1a412f3efaa0f371da8e8c89f4975.

9. Stefano Harney and Fred Moten, *The Undercommons: Fugitive Planning and Black Study* (Minor Compositions, 2013), 1.
10. Love, *Educational Freedom*, 11.
11. Love, *Educational Freedom*, 101.
12. Love, *Educational Freedom*, 70.
13. Joy Buolamwini, "AI, Ain't I a Woman?," MIT Black History, 2018, https://www.blackhistory.mit.edu/archive/joy-buolamwini-ai-aint-i-woman-2018.
14. While we realize the medium of a printed or digital book may not easily support video, we encourage you to view the video of Dr. Buolamwini sharing her spoken word poem.
15. Joy Buolamwini, *Unmasking AI: My Mission to Protect What is Human in a World of Machines* (Random House, 2023).
16. Safiya Umoja Noble, "Algorithms of Oppression: How Search Engines Reinforce Racism," in *Algorithms of Oppression* (New York University Press, 2018).
17. ChatGPT, response to "show me images of Black hair," OpenAI, October 11, 2024, https://chat.openai.com/chat.
18. Connected Learning Alliance, "The Race, Abolition, and AI Program: Empowering Young People to Navigate the Intersection of Race and Technology," 2024, https://connectedwellbeing.org/case-study-the-race-abolition-and-ai-program/.
19. Connected Learning Alliance, "Race, Abolition, and AI."
20. Julia Delacroix, "Teaching Hard History from the Beginning: Children Should Learn About American Slavery Starting in Kindergarten," *Southern Poverty Law Center: Learning for Justice*, no. 63 (2019), https://www.learningforjustice.org/magazine/fall-2019/teaching-hard-history-from-the-beginning.
21. Ida B. Wells Just Data Lab, "About," Just Data Lab website, 2021, https://www.thejustdatalab.com/about.
22. Bridget Todd, host, *IRL: Online Life is Real Life*, podcast, "AI from Above," August 15, 2022, https://2022.internethealthreport.org/episodes/ai-from-above/.
23. Algorithmic Justice League (AJL), "The CRASH Project," AJL website, 2024, https://www.ajl.org/crash-project.
24. Algorithmic Justice League, "Get Ready to Drag the Cistem," AJL website, 2024, https://www.ajl.org/drag-vs-ai.
25. Twin Cities Innovation Alliance (TCIA), "About TCIA," TCIA website, 2024, https://www.tciamn.org/about.
26. Detroit Community Technology Project (DCTP), official DCTP website, 2024, https://detroitcommunitytech.org/.
27. Detroit Community Technology Project, " To: The Michigan House and Senate. Protect Our Privacy! No More Surveillance for People in Michigan!," OrganizeFor, 2019, https://campaigns.organizefor.org/petitions/protect-our-privacy-no-more-surveillance-for-people-in-michigan.

28. Myrtle Thompson-Curtis, "Green Chairs Not Green Lights: Building Community From Our Front Porches," *Riverwise: Special Surveillance Issue* (August 2019), https://detroitcommunitytech.org/system/tdf/librarypdfs/2019-2206_Riverwise-Surveillance.pdf?file=1&type=node&id=80&force=0&force=.
29. Lynn Ma, "The Anti-social Network: These Teens Are Ditching Instagram, Snapchat and TikTok," *Chalkbeat New York*, December 15, 2022, https://www.chalkbeat.org/newyork/2022/12/15/23511604/nyc-schools-students-social-media-smartphones-luddite-club/.
30. Brian Merchant, *Blood in the Machine: The Origins of the Rebellion Against Big Tech* (Little, Brown, 2023).
31. Dara Kerr, "Armed with Traffic Cones, Protesters Are Immobilizing Driverless Cars," *NPR Business*, August 26, 2023, https://www.npr.org/2023/08/26/1195695051/driverless-cars-san-francisco-waymo-cruise5.
32. Xinyue Li, Zhenpeng Chen, Jie M. Zhang, Federica Sarro, Ying Zhang, and Xuanzhe Liu, "Dark-Skin Individuals Are at More Risk on the Street: Unmasking Fairness Issues of Autonomous Driving Systems," arXiv preprint (2023), https://arxiv.org/abs/2308.02935.
33. Adam Jacobson, "Hong Kong Protesters Use Laser Pointers to Deter Police, Scramble Facial Recognition," *CBC News*, August 11, 2019, https://www.cbc.ca/news/world/hong-kong-protest-lasers-facial-recognition-technology-1.5240651.

CHAPTER 6

1. Patricia Hill Collins, *Black Feminist Thought* (Hyman, 2002), 223.
2. National Security Alliance, "Manage Your Privacy Settings," May 26, 2022, https://staysafeonline.org/resources/manage-your-privacy-settings/.
3. Page with sign-up link for The Privacy Paradox newsletter and podcast series (*Note to Self* special series), The Privacy Paradox website, 2017, https://project.wnyc.org/privacy-paradox/.
4. *Note to Self*, podcast, "The Privacy Paradox," 5-episode special series, WNYC Studios, 2017, https://project.wnyc.org/privacy-paradox/.
5. Google Account Help, "How Do I Access & Control My Google Activity?," Google Help website, https://support.google.com/accounts/answer/7028918?hl=en&co=GENIE.Platform%3DDesktop.
6. Zachary McAuliffe, "5 Reasons You Should Use DuckDuckGo Instead of Google," *CNET*, September 2, 2023, https://www.cnet.com/tech/services-and-software/five-reasons-you-should-use-duckduckgo-instead-of-google/.
7. The National Conference of State Legislators (NCSL), "Artificial Intelligence 2024 Legislation," website of the NCSL, September 9, 2024, https://www.ncsl.org/technology-and-communication/artificial-intelligence-2024-legislation.
8. Shana V. White, Allison Scott, and Sonia Koshy, *Responsible AI and Tech Justice: A Guide for K-12 Education* (Kapor Foundation, 2024), 1, https://kaporfoundation

.org/wp-content/uploads/2024/01/FINAL-FULL-GUIDE-kapor-foundation-responsible-ai.pdf.

9. White et al., *Responsible AI,* 5.
10. Jessica Shiller and the BMORE Caucus, "Winning in Baltimore: The Story of How BMORE Put Racial Equity at the Center of Teacher Union Organizing," *Berkeley Review of Education* 9, no. 1 (2019).
11. The National Education Association (NEA), "The Six Pillars of Community Schools Toolkit," website of the NEA, 2020, https://www.nea.org/sites/default/files/2020-06/Comm%20Schools%20ToolKit-final%20digi-web-72617.pdf.

ACKNOWLEDGMENTS

STEPHANIE

To the Budhai, Smith, and Macon family, thank you for your unwavering patience, love, and support.

Thank you to my amazing coauthor, Marie, who has shared her gifts, time, and spirit with me; I am forever grateful to you.

Thank you, Karen, for reaching out to me and getting us started on this impactful journey, and being a steady thought partner.

To the incomparable Punya Mishra, thank you for connecting with our work and crafting an inspiring foreword.

And to all of the educators and creators of StoryAI, thank you for sharing vignettes with examples of using AI for justice and joy in K–12 classrooms.

MARIE

First and always, a heartfelt thank you to my family who cheer me on and make time and space for me to do this work. Thank you also to Stephanie, for trusting me as a writing partner and friend. Thanks to Punya for writing the foreword and always being game to think creatively and with his trademark warmth. Thank you to our editor, Karen, and her encouraging words and incisive vision for the book. I could not have done this without you all.

ABOUT THE AUTHORS

STEPHANIE SMITH BUDHAI (she/her) is an Associate Professor in the Educational Technology program at the University of Delaware and is the recipient of an Excellence in Teacher Education Award from the International Society for Technology in Education (ISTE). She is a council chair for the Society for Information Technology and Teacher Education (SITE) and has published over eighty practitioner articles for Tech & Learning and eight books to support teaching, learning, and technology in education. She holds K–12 teaching certifications in technology education, instructional technology, elementary education, and special education.

MARIE K. HEATH (she/her) is not a robot, but she refuses to prove it to Google's CAPTCHA. She currently works as an Associate Professor of Learning Design and Technology at Loyola University Maryland. Prior to her work in higher education, Marie taught high school social studies in Baltimore County Public Schools. Her scholarship interrogates schools and technologies as current sites of encoded oppression, and labors to advance more just technological and educational futures. She is coeditor of the *CITE Social Studies Journal*, cofounder of the Civics of Technology project, and a faculty fellow at the Center for Leadership and Social Justice Education at Loyola University Maryland. If you ask generative AI a question about Marie, it replies with the Mariah Carey "I don't know her" meme.

INDEX